Small Town Jubilee: Beccles in 1897

E.A.Goodwyn

The Boydell Press . Ipswich

Published by The Boydell Press Ltd
P.O. Box 24, Ipswich IP1 1JJ

ISBN 0 85115 053 5

Printed in Great Britain by
Dramrite Printers Ltd, Long Lane, London SE1

To Dr E.S.NICHOLSON

Chairman of The Beccles Society

CONTENTS

Small Advertisements from the Beccles and district weekly newspaper, *The East Suffolk Gazette* and *Humour of the Year* reprinted in the newspaper from various magazines, interspersed between chapters.

ACKNOWLEDGMENT

I wish to thank the Editors of *The East Anglian Magazine* for permission to quote from articles by A.E.Pye and F.C.Oakley.

INTRODUCTION

HENRY JAMES WAS keenly sensitive to the qualities of a town. When he made Beccles in Suffolk the home of the admirable Mr Longdon, in "The Awkward Age", he paid the town a considerable compliment. Mr Longdon, his house and his garden are represented as an ideal of English provincial culture. Though the model for this house is thought to have been James's own home in Rye, Sussex, there were in 1897, when James was in Suffolk and was planning his novel, several Georgian houses in Beccles with fine walled gardens, which could have served him equally as well. "Beyond the lawn the house was before him, old, square, red-roofed, well assured of its right to the place it took up in the world. This was a considerable space— in the little world, at least, of Beccles— and the look of possession had everywhere mixed with it, in the form of old windows, and doors, the tone of old red surfaces, the age of old high creepers, the long confirmation of time."

A few years before James chose Beccles for Mr Longdon, James Hissey had found the church in its splendid setting an architectural ideal for the small English town. "So boldly does the church uprise above the clustering houses, with such a masterful air does it assert its dignity, that Beccles seems more like a miniature cathedral city than a little-known provincial town."

Was Beccles then, at the end of the nineteenth century, a town of traditional gentility and architectural charm? There were other contrasting features, including four large Nonconformist Victorian churches. The Nonconformists were numerous. Matthew Arnold's strictures on Victorian nonconformity were perhaps exaggerated— "a life of jealousy of the Establishment, disputes, tea-meetings, openings of chapels, sermons...and, in the evening, for a great treat, a lecture on Teetotalism or Nunneries. Can any life be imagined more hideous, more dismal, more unenviable?" These were, in fact, features of Nonconformist life in Beccles— and A.E.Pye's account of Sunday afternoons completes a picture of lugubrious piety: "A walk round the town or a visit to the local cemetery was the chief form of exercise. All the latest graves were inspected, the wreaths and flowers admired and the captions on the attached cards eagerly scanned. Comments, adverse and favourable, on the departed individual were freely exchanged. All the relatives of the deceased person, dressed in deep mourning, would gather round the grave."

The morning service at the Parish Church— James sent Mr Longdon with one of his London guests to the afternoon service— was a social occasion. Gentlemen might wear top hats and kid gloves. The Nonconformists too had their social distinctions at chapel, for the ground floor was occupied by the well-to-do employer class or tradespeople, whilst working people and servants sat in the gallery. They had a compensation; no collection was taken there.

Important as the denominational aspect of religion still was in 1897— and at this time the Roman Catholic resurgence in the town focused attention upon it— an adequate picture of life in Beccles must include several quite different features. There was, for instance, the curious prevalence of nicknames for well-known characters. There were "Chitty" Crickmore, the horse dealer, "Hopper" Clutten (who claimed a knowledge of secret cures inherited from his gipsy mother), the wherryman "Rat" Goffin and his two sons "Toasty" and "Wappity", three Woolners— "Chowty", "Honey" and "Scanty"— and, amongst others, the chimney-sweep Walter Rose, whose nickname of "Tongy" this anecdote illustrates. "Tongy" had been asked by the wife of a very important person in the town to do a particular job at their house. A few days later the husband, driving in his horse and cart, and meeting "Tongy" carrying his sweep's brush and bag of soot on his back, reined up and enquired: "Who told you to do that job up at the house?"

"Yar ow' woman," "Tongy" replied rudely, whereat the husband angrily slashed his whip across "Tongy's" shoulders. Without further ado, "Tongy" retaliated by pushing his soot brushes into the face of the irate husband.

If Beccles was a place of very mixed public manners, it was also a place of surprisingly mixed employment for a small country town. On the one hand there were in 1897 the crafts, industries and businesses of a rural economy— the coach-builder, the wheelwright, the gun-smith, blacksmiths, saddlers; three mills; Samuel Field, agricultural implement maker; the Vulcan agricultural engineering works; the tannery of J.K. and W.H.Garrod, built near the river for convenience of getting oak bark by water; and the large maltings of John Crisp and Son. There was the Stock Mart of Messrs Read, Stanford and Gayford, whose catalogue for the 29th annual Michaelmas sale of horses and colts contained 300 items, buyers coming from London and all parts of the country; and at whose Stock Sale in December some 40 grazing beasts, 115 sheep, 80 pigs, cows, calves, turkeys and ducks were sold for the Christmas market.

Rural interests were also evident in local societies. The Poultry Society was the largest and its fourth Annual Show at the Corn Hall in November attracted 300 exhibitors of whom 33 were Beccles residents. Of the 87 classes, 41 were for pigeons.

On the other hand, there were industries not directly related to rural life— the large printing works of Messrs Clowes and Sons and the engineering works of Elliott and Garrood, whose first compound marine engine was about to come into successful service. It is noteworthy also that the Cooperative Society was well established and in 1897 had 700 members.

The two private schools for boys, both part-boarding, were significantly different. The Fauconberge School had a traditional classical curriculum, whereas the relatively new Beccles College offered an education with a commercial bias— though both put much emphasis on games. And both must have contributed to the relative prosperity of Beccles, whose population had increased from 5,721 in 1881 to 6,669 in 1891 at a time when East Anglian towns were generally declining. Agriculture was in the throes of the long depression. In spite of this, East Anglia celebrated the Diamond Jubilee with an optimistic enthusiasm notably strong in Beccles, where a local printer produced his own version of the long and glorious reign.

What was the impact upon the town of all "the tumult and the shouting"? Perhaps the influence upon the children was most important. The shopkeepers had some extra trade; the civic dignitaries had their public occasions; energetic organisers enjoyed their special opportunities; but the children were made the centre of it all. In all the preparations, the feasting, the entertainments, the giving of momentoes, two ideas were constantly put before them: the greatness of Britain and the goodness of the Queen.

There was also a unifying social influence, tending to soften the harsh sectarian differences which were a marked feature of the town. When, a few weeks before the Celebration, Lester Drummond addressed a large audience in the Old Market Place upon the highly provocative topic: "Why I believe in an Infallible Pope", he was subjected to a barrage of questions; and when asked, quite seriously, "Who is the rightful occupant of the English throne— the Pope or Queen Victoria?" he replied: "The Queen— God bless her!" A storm of applause greeted this answer. The meeting dispersed in high good humour.

Small Advertisements

WANTED. *In Beccles Hospital, a steady, respectable person as* COOK. *Some housework required. Must have good character. Wages £12, and all found except beer.*

WANTED. *A good* PLAIN COOK: *soups, fish, game etc., good bread; a church-woman; assistance given—Mrs Rant, Chediston Hall, Halesworth.*

WANTED. *Active* YOUNG MEN, *between 18 and 25 years of age to join the* ARMY. *Good prospects for intelligent and well-conducted young men. Apply to Sergt-Inst.J.Smyth, The Armoury, Old Market, Beccles.*

WANTED. *Gooseberries, Raspberries, Red Currants, Black Currants, in various quantities: Deliveries to R.D.Wilkinson, Jam Manufacturer, Beccles*

340 ACRES PARTRIDGE SHOOTING *to Feb. Good supply of Birds. Easy rail distance—Mr Reston West, Toft Monks, Beccles*

WAVENEY HOTEL, *Beccles. Summer resort for visitors. Private sitting-rooms, bedrooms, etc., good selection of open sailing and rowing boats on hire. A Bowling Green has been laid down from the Hotel to the River-side Pleasure Gardens where good Luncheons and Teas can be provided.*

MOURNING *and* MEMORIAL CARDS *printed at the Caxton Press, Beccles.*

1. THE IMPORTANCE OF BEING LOCAL

"The next business," said the Mayor, "is the appointment of a surveyor."

The quarterly meeting of the Town Council on the evening of January 11th had already dealt with many matters: the allocation of another policeman to the town; the report of the sub-committee on sewage disposal; the finances of the Bathing-Place: the report of the Fire Brigade; the repairs to Denmark Road, said to be in "a disgraceful state"; the appointment of tradesmen for the quarter— blacksmith, carpenter, grocer, wheelwright, iron-monger, painter and harness-maker; and the Medical Officer's Report, which mentioned eleven cases of diphtheria and forty-two of scarlet fever (none fatal, however), during the preceding six months. All this and other business had been completed.

"There are fifty-eight applications," the Mayor continued, "and I do not know how they are to be taken."

Alderman Rix, solicitor and banker of long experience and ready tongue, had an immediate proposal: read the names and testimonials only of those applicants any member might wish to have read. Most of them knew for whom they intended to vote. He would also propose that, instead of having a show of hands, each member should write down on a piece of paper the name of the person he wished to see elected. Then these papers should be handed to the Mayor.

This proposal invited a most unusual procedure. But the Alderman had an important reason. The matter was unusually delicate. Of those fifty-eight applicants, four were local men— and of these, one was a relative of the Mayor and another the son of Councillor Woodroffe!

Alderman Masters thought the proposal unfair to the applicants. The applications and the testimonials of all should be read and any candidate getting a single vote should stand again in a second poll.

The Town Clerk: "Am I to read simply the names of the applicants?"

The Mayor: "Names and testimonials as well."

The Clerk read the application and five testimonials of the first man, with twenty years experience as assistant surveyor at Newcastle. Then he exclaimed. "It will take three hours to get through this whole mass of papers!" At this, Alderman Rix repeated his proposal and finally it was agreed that the Clerk should give merely the name and qualifications of each applicant as concisely as possible.

The local candidates were: Messrs L.T.Clarkson, E.J.Hindes A.S.L., A.Pells F.S.I. and T.W.Woodroffe. Among the other candidates were several town surveyors and assistant surveyors, civil engineers, sanitary inspectors and engineers, from as far afield as East Ham, Cardiff, Birmingham, Southampton, South Shields, Manchester and the Isle of Wight. When the applicants had been made known, papers were handed round. Each member wrote the name of the man he wished to see elected. The clerk collected the papers and the Mayor announced the voting:

T.W.Woodroffe 8
A.Pells 5
E.J.Hindes 2

Not a single vote had been cast for a non-local candidate!

The election of T.W.Woodroffe was proposed, seconded and carried nem.con. Councillor Woodroffe thanked the Council for the election of his son.

"I have no fear but he will fulfil the duties to your satisfaction." (Applause) The meeting closed at 10 p.m.

In the same issue as the long account of the council's proceedings appeared the first indignant protests:

THE SURVEYORSHIP

Sir,

Is it possible that the gross piece of nepotism just perpetrated by a public body in Beccles, will be allowed to pass over without protest, united and strong, on the part of the rate-payers? I feel constrained to express the utter amazement called forth by the appointment, over the heads of many fully qualified men of ripe experience, of a young untried man to fill the responsible post of surveyor to this borough, etc.

AN INDIGNANT BURGESS

MUNICIPAL JOBBERY

Sir,

The latest phase of local *mis*-management and misapplication of public money has surely been exhibited by the Town Council in this appointment of a Surveyor! This office has been given to a young and inexperienced man, son of a councillor,— a junior, I am told, among the large number of qualified applicants— an act which can only be stigmatised as a gross abuse of privilege by some unworthy representatives of the burgesses trust etc.

NEMESIS

"NEMESIS" (who was to write again when the next local election was due) and another correspondent, "JEHU", hinted broadly that Masonic influence had been exercised. The following week the chorus of protest continued. One heavily sarcastic letter began:

Dear Mr Editor,

I think your correspondents last week were much too hard on our new town surveyor. The young man, it is true, has only just left school, and does not know about anything except football: but then, we must all learn, and I feel sure the ratepayers will be only too glad to pay him £100 a year, for the next few years, while he learns his duties. Besides, I understand he wants to get married...."

RATEPAYER

A week later, the paper published a list purporting to show how each member of the Council had voted. It did not disclose how this list was obtained, but the list was not disputed.

A proposal was now canvassed in the town— its opponents alleged the idea was hatched in a pub— to present a memorial to the Council for the cancellation of the appointment. The memorial, with 104 signatures, was duly presented and the question of its consideration placed upon the agenda of a special meeting on March 1st.

Meanwhile, an old custom had been revived. Various "squibs" on the matter were circulated. One of these favoured young Woodroffe and poked fun at Councillor Buck (who had voted for Pells) and at Alderman Wilson, formidable Scottish manager of the Caxton Printing Works and Colonel of the local Artillery volunteers, who, unaccountably, had not attended the fateful meeting.

THE DEATH OF BECCLES

"My Buckey lad", said Colonel Grand,
"One thing I cannot understand:
How dared the Council, 'gainst my will,
Appoint Surveyor, Woodroffe Bill?"
"Grand Sir, (here Buckey winked one eye),
"Some venom in our ink we'll try,
For vile indeed must be the men
To act against our will, ye ken!"
"Then up and at them, Buckey dear,
For you have none but me to fear.
So, Buckey, get some letters writ,

No matter who they sting or hit!"
Alas! anathema was hurled
Against our little Beccles world;
Our glory gone, our honour lost!
And at a most terrific cost!
Ye shades departed, hear our cry,
And tell, oh! tell us wherefore! Why?
A spirit whispered in the air,
'The gallant Colonel was not there
On that disastrous evil day,
When all that's good was thrown away;
And yet not all, there still remains
A young Surveyor, with some brains,
With will to work, and health in store,
He wants fair play, and nothing more.'

'Old Hundred'

More seriously, an article appeared in "The Surveyor", under the heading "THE BECCLES SCANDAL". This was re-printed in the local paper. The article castigated the entire proceedings of the Council and described the appointment as "a very glaring piece of jobbery". A final sarcasm was reserved for Councillor Woodroffe's speech of thanks— "the farce reached its height when the fond, but evidently thick-skinned, parent solemnly rose to his feet and delivered himself of this tasteful and appropriate utterance etc".

At the Council meeting on March 1st, the Town Clerk read the memorial, which ended "For these and other reasons your memorialists pray the Council will revoke the appointment made, and elect some person qualified to perform the duties in a competent and satisfactory manner".

Alderman Rix, who had not voted for Woodroffe, at once rose and, in his most persuasive manner, urged that the memorial be not considered. His views on matters of procedure always carried weight, as one of two solicitors on the Council. The Mayor was a miller, the Deputy Mayor a chemist, others included a wine and spirit merchant, an ironmoner, a grocer, a butcher and two builders, Councillor Woodroffe being one. Rix argued that it was essential for the officers of the Council to be independent and not to fear that they could be dismissed when some burgesses could be got to sign a memorial. "We must not allow that to take place under any circumstances."

Councillor Larkman, the other solicitor, seconded.

But Councillor Buck had his say— "the appointment was ill-advised and ill-considered"— proposing three months' notice to Woodroffe. He found a seconder, but no other support. The motion "That the Council decline to consider the memorial" was carried by ten votes to two.

Young Woodroffe soon proved acceptable. The success of Beccles Caxton in winning the Suffolk Senior Cup was a great help in a town where football enthusiasm ran high— he was the captain. And later in the year, at one of the public dinners (those functions so useful for healing, with a dash of unction, local differences) his work as Surveyor received praise from more than one speaker. He responded with well-judged diffidence. But there was to be a sequel, when the next local elections were held in November.

2. THE WRONG SIDE OF THE LAW

MR HENRY BOYCE, headmaster of the Leman School, was an early riser. Whilst taking a solitary walk on a Sunday morning in January, and passing the shop in Hungate Street of Mr Bowles, jeweller and watchmaker, he nearly fell over one of the shutters, which was lying across the path. He looked at the window and saw the lower pane of glass evidently cut, the corners pushed through. There being no constable about, he went to the Police Station and called Inspector Lingley. It was then about 5.25 a.m.

About £100 worth of jewellery had been stolen—30 watches, 33 ladies rings, 33 wedding rings and a variety of small gold and silver articles. Five men appeared at Beccles Police Court on charges concerning the theft. Two were at once discharged for lack of evidence and a third, who admitted some complicity, was discharged so that he could appear as a prosecution witness. This man was James Sampson, labourer. He told a long story of how one of the other two, Stephen Oxborough, an ex-convict, had asked him to join in the robbery, but he, on the persuasion of his sister-in-law, had declined. Subsequently he went with Oxborough and the other prisoner, Charles Sheppard, to the Common, where the haul of jewellery was hidden in a tin, inside a hole made with a trowel. They gave him two watches and two gold rings, which he later sold to "Toasty" Goffin, a fish-hawker; and Goffin sold the rings to Charles Hollis of Yarmouth, a razor-grinder. The rings eventually found their way to a Yarmouth pawn-broker.

Oxborough and Sheppard were committed for trial at the Assizes at Ipswich. But here a different picture of what had happened emerged. The two accused protested that they had both been in bed on the night in question. Oxborough slept in William Goffin's fish-house, which was always kept locked at night, "in case the herring should walk", as Goffin said. The room was secured by a bar on the outside, which could not be removed from inside; and there was a sheer drop of over forty feet to the ground. There was also a dog in the yard, which would have barked if anyone had come out. The other accused, Sheppard, a tramp, who sang and played a tin whistle in public houses, had slept at the Queen's Head on the night of the robbery. The landlord said Sheppard had gone to bed at 11 p.m. Another man and a lad slept in the same room. He did not think Sheppard could possibly have got out of the pub without someone noticing.

The only evidence against the accused was the uncorroborated story of Sampson. The Judge indicated to the Jury that there was insufficient evidence to warrant conviction; the Jury after only a few minutes consideration found the accused not guilty. And so Oxborough and Sheppard were both acquitted, and Sampson also escaped any prosecution by having turned Queen's evidence! There were some clever rogues about somewhere. Mr Bowles, however, recovered most of the stolen goods.

Oxborough was less fortunate later in the year. On Jubilee Day he entered Honington Hall lodge whilst the occupants were enjoying the village festivities, and stole ten shillings and some clothes; and a few days later he took a coat, waistcoat and three shirts from Ellingham Rectory. Finding the door open, he just walked in and took the things, being unable, as he said, to resist the temptation. So back to prison he went.

A linen-line in a garden near the river was too great a temptation for Beccles wherrymen, Henry Chilvers and Lewis Clark. Suspicion falling on these two men who had passed the place in a wherry on their return from Norwich, Inspector Lingley went to Chilvers' house in Newgate Street and found some of the things stolen from the linen-line in a box in the bedroom. P.C.Leftly then intercepted Chilvers near the Parish Church and found he was carrying a bundle with more of the missing property. A search of the wherry revealed some more. They had taken fifteen articles of clothing, sheets, towels, and pillowslips.

Poaching was, of course, still a frequent offence. Sometimes there were encounters between poachers and gamekeepers. James Raven, gamekeeper to Sir Charles Clarke at Ellough, gave evidence of a case in February. One night in the previous October he heard shots fired in a wood about a mile away. He got to within a few hundred yards of the wood, concealed himself in a fence and soon saw two men approaching. They walked down and did not see him till he came out and said "Helloa, you have had some fair shots!" They said "Oh!" and bolted down the fence. Raven followed. When they jumped the fence, he got hold of the older man Samuel Roofe— of whom we shall hear again in this chapter and in "A Policeman's Lot was not a Peaceful One"— and as they scuffled on the ground, Roofe struck him a blow on the forehead with a stick, which half unsensed him. He went down to report to Beccles Police Station. Roofe tried unsuccessfully to prove mistaken identity. He was sentenced to 14 days hard labour for the poaching offence and 7 days for the assult.

Prosecutions for cruelty to animals were fairly frequent. There were two cases of cruelty to ponies in October, one involving Samuel Roofe, who was sent to gaol for another 21 days hard labour. At the same time there were two cases of assault and two of "drunk and disorderly". The previous month, Alfred Borrett, the landlord of the White Lion, was charged with cruelty to a horse, in unusual circumstances. There was a party at Benacre Hall, and a large van of eatables was brought down from London to Beccles by rail. Borrett undertook to horse the van on the remainder of the journey by road, and used two light hackneys for that purpose. The weight of the van was 2 tons 10 cwt and the distance about seven miles. About two miles from Benacre the horses became very distressed. Borrett, who was behind in a four-wheeler with six waiters, was heard to urge on the driver of the van. Evidence was given of one horse having a raw wound on the side. Borrett was fined one guinea.

Cases of non-attendance at school were frequent. There were, for instance, six cases on August 3rd. A fine of 2s.6d. was the usual penalty. Refusals to vaccinate children occurred several times; the magistrates expressed sympathy for these conscientious objectors, but had to impose the fine of one pound.

In August, too, there was a typical case of assult in a drunken brawl at the Ship Inn. It started when several men— including two who were nut-hawkers— came in and started to sing a song. Other men were talking. One of the singers shouted: "You fat-headed old— , shut your mouth!" In the fracas that ensued, kicks and punches were exchanged, and blood flowed freely. Evidence in court was confused and conflicting.

Boys were in trouble now and then. Two were fined for shooting stones at a lamp with catapults, and two for playing football, to the annoyance of pedestrians, in the New Market.

Occasional glimpses of poor working conditions emerge from prosecutions under the Factory Acts, as when Walter Fenn, tailor, was fined 25s for having three apprentices with him in a small workshop of 500 cubic feet; the Acts required 250 cubic feet per person.

There were tramps who had to find somewhere to sleep. One December night, Cornelius White was found sleeping in the stable of Mr Cleveland, veterinary surgeon. He had turned the horse out of the stable to have undisturbed possession of a good bed of straw; but Mr Cleveland, hearing the horse moving about, got up to secure it. P.C. Leftly was called and found White soundly asleep on the straw. The unlucky tramp was taken to the Police Station and later sentenced to seven days hard labour.

Humour of the Year

LOCATING HIM: *"Seen my boy Tommy anywhere, Mrs Rook?" - "No, I ain't seen 'im, but there's a fight at the other end of the street."*

HE WENT OFF: *Sturdy mendicant: "Please spare me a copper, sir." Benevolent old gentleman: "Certainly, my man. There's one just coming around the corner."*

IN THE EAST END: *Little Georgie: "Mamma dear, is this dirty place what they call the East?" - Mama: "Yes, darling." Little Georgie: "Then I don't wonder the wise men came from it."*

IN OUR FREE LIBRARY: *"Anything in the papers today, Billy?" "No, only five divorces, two separations, and one scandal in high life. Them aristocrats have been goin' bloomin' slow just lately, ain't they?"*

3. THE JUBILEE: TIME FOR SUGGESTIONS

ALL OVER THE country, in city, town and village, public meetings were called, proposals made, committees appointed. Argument centred round the questions: Should the occasion be celebrated by a permanent memorial or by a communal feasting— or both? How should the money be raised? How should it be allocated?

In East Anglia, many and various were the proposals urged at meetings in March, April, May and June: at Downham, a gallery for the Town Hall; at Wells, conversion of the old life-boat house into a reading and refreshment room; at Walsingham, restoration of the church clock; at Great Dunham, a hand hearse for that straggling parish; at Hilgay, a chestnut tree on the village green with seats round it; at Dereham, Swimming Baths— or a stained glass window in memory of the poet Cowper; at Woolpit, a new well to be sunk; at Woodbridge, a swimming bath; at Felixstowe, one or two shelters on the beach. At Wells, where six almshouses or a fire engine were suggested, a bricklayer's labourer proposed— a feast. Feasting the poor at times of national rejoicing was a strong tradition. And everywhere this tradition was upheld by majority opinion. A packed meeting at North Walsham attended with "much humorous disorder" heard three suggestions— repair of the Town Cross, feeding the aged poor, a new fence to the Recreation Ground— and then a young man enquired whether there would be any sports. Immediately came shouts from the audience: "Sports! We don't want no sports; feed the whole on us!"

Plenty of time was given for the people of Beccles to consider their plans. A Public Meeting in the Town Hall was arranged for Tuesday March 16th— the Mayor, of course, as Chairman— "To consider what steps shall be taken by the Inhabitants of Beccles to COMMEMORATE the SIXTIETH YEAR of the

REIGN of Her Majesty the QUEEN."

The Town Hall was full when the proceedings began with the singing of a verse of the National Anthem. Then the Mayor addressed the meeting. He spoke first of Victoria's reign and the world-wide celebrations in preparation, concluding this part of his speech: "It is well, when we consider that no sovereign has ever ruled so long, and no monarch has ever ruled so well or so gloriously, and that during the Queen's reign the privileges and blessings of peace and prosperity, of liberty and freedom have been so liberally dispensed— it is well that we should, if possible, commemorate and hand down to our children's children some memento which will lead them to say at least that we of this generation were a loyal and patriotic people" (Cheers). Calling for suggestions before the selection of a Jubilee committee, he gave reasons for the project he himself favoured— a new Town Hall.

Mr B.Revell, landlord of the Railway Inn, thought there was one thing more desirable than a new Town Hall, and that was a sanatorium for contagious diseases. They had nearly all got families, and none of them knew what a day might bring forth. Diphtheria, scarlet fever, smallpox or typhoid fever might attack them, and then they would find the great convenience of having a sanatorium.

Mr W.Read, auctioneer and land agent, objected that both proposals would require money from the rates and that was not right. (Hear, hear). He suggested the building of almshouses for six aged women. The cost would be about £1000, but no permanent endowment would be necessary, as the almshouses could be handed over to the Town Feoffees to be maintained from the funds.

Col.Wilson, Manager of Clowes Printing Works, favoured the idea of providing a sleeping room for the head nurse at the Hospital.

Father Fulton thought any memorial must be paid

for by voluntary subscriptions; a new Town Hall, a sanatorium and almshouses would cost more than Beccles could raise in that way.

Mr H.Copeman, butcher, supported the idea of almshouses. "And I hope something will be done to ensure that the old people and children have a treat." (Cheers).

Canon Rowsell, the Rector, proposed the nomination of a committee consisting of the Mayor and Corporation, heads of friendly societies and ministers of religion in the town and such other persons as might be named at the meeting, to consider all the suggestions. He added to these the idea of starting a fund by which a sick nurse might be provided to visit the homes of the poor. "Many towns smaller than Beccles have such a useful person, and it is certainly a want we are experiencing here."

A committee was then nominated. Members of the School Board, the Burial Board, the Feoffees and ten other prominent citizens were added to those mentioned by the Rector.

Mr Alfred Hockey, joint Principal of Beccles College, suggested that the people of Beccles should be invited to send postcards to the Town Clerk indicating their preferences. He himself favoured the idea of a new Town Hall. "People who have come to Beccles to give good concerts or theatrical performances have given the Town Hall the name of 'The Actors' Grave'." (Laughter). It was unhealthy and inconvenient, as many of those present could testify.

The postcards idea led to a further discussion. Mr Rix, solicitor and bank manager, suggested that they should state how much money they were going to give. (Hisses). Mr Walton, wine and spirit merchant, remarked: "You won't get many postcards." The idea, however, was adopted. A week was to be allowed for the sending in of cards; after that the committee would meet; and then the Mayor was

to call another public meeting.
Three cheers were given for the Mayor, and the meeting concluded, as it had begun, with the first verse of the National Anthem, heartily sung.

The Jubilee: Small Advertisements

VICTORIA QUEEN EMPRESS! *Beautiful* ALUMINIUM *calendar medals representing Her Majesty in 1837 and 1897. 1/2 per doz: 7/9 per 100. Samples 2½d post free. Bertie-Smith, Pinefield Ave. Forest Hill, London.*

JUBILEE CELEBRATIONS PRESENTATION BUILDINGS *for every purpose, erected any distance, fit for immediate occupation. Churches, Chapels, and Club-rooms a speciality. Write for designs and inclusive estimates. Humphries Ltd. Iron Building Contractors, Knightsbridge, London S.W.*

4. A LOSS TO THE TOWN

EDWARD BOWLES CROWFOOT M.B., Medical Officer of Health for Beccles, had been under considerable strain during the early weeks of 1897. His assistant was unwell; his elder brother and partner, William Miller Crowfoot, had been enjoined absolute rest and had gone to Eastbourne. It was, as always, a strenuous time of the year for doctors.

The Crowfoots were the best known family in Beccles. William Crowfoot, merchant, had come to Beccles early in the eighteenth century; his grandson, also William, was the first to become a doctor, establishing a family practice which continued throughout the nineteenth century. The Crowfoots had a long record of public service. The list of Portreeves and Feoffees of Beccles has innumerable Crowfoot entries; and after the passing of the Municipal Reform Act in 1835, they served as mayors:

1836-37	William Henchman Crowfoot
1839-40)	
1840-41)	William John Crowfoot
1843-44	William Henchman Crowfoot
1845-46	William Edward Crowfoot
1851-52	William John Crowfoot
1852-53)	
1853-54)	William Edward Crowfoot
1875-76	William Miller Crowfoot
1881-82	William Miller Crowfoot

In a small town like Beccles, with its numerous societies and the requirements of a borough, great demands were made upon a man of means, intellect and wide interests, with a strong sense of public duty and a partiality for local prominence. In 1897 W.M.Crowfoot had ceased to be an Alderman, but he continued to fulfil numerous public duties.

He was a Magistrate, a Churchwarden, a Feoffee, Chairman of the School Board, Hon.Medical Officer to the Hospital, a Trustee of the Fauconberge

School, a Governor of the Leman School, and a committee member of the Eastern Counties Asylum, of the Library, and the R.S.P.C.A. He was a Director of the Beccles Water and Gas Company. Besides all this, he was a keen entomologist, had lectured to local organisations on popular sciences, and had written an erudite paper on "Beccles Street Names".

The younger brother was not a public man. His time and energy had been devoted to medicine. He was Medical Officer to most of the local friendly socities; and known as a great friend of the poor.

On the evening of Friday February 12th he had been attending patients to a late hour, so that he had little sleep; but he was on duty at the surgery as usual the following morning. A few minutes after he had returned home, a servant found him prostrate on his bed. Heart failure had caused his death, at the age of 51.

The news soon spread through the town. "Poor gentleman," said a woman, "there'll not be a house in Beccles where a tear will not be shed for Mr Edward."

The elaborate funeral accorded with Victorian ideas of public respect to a worthy representative of such a family. In nearly every house the blinds were drawn. The muffled bell tolled solemnly as the mourners assembled and the long cortege marched to the Parish Church. The procession was headed by the Mayor, Aldermen and Councillors, preceded by the pall bearer, with draped maces. The Town Clerk and Borough Treasurer were in black robes. There were four family mourning carriages and a fifth for the family servants. As the cortege left for the concluding part of the service at the cemetery, the "Dead March" in Saul was played on the organ. There were forty-eight floral tributes.

In the evening muffled peals were rung on the church bells by the Beccles company of ringers.

A month after the death of Edward Crowfoot,

when suggestions for the permanent Jubilee memorial were under discussion at public meetings, W.M.Crowfoot wrote to the Mayor: "It is the intention of my brother, my sister and myself, to endow, in memory of my brother Edward, a parish nurse whose services will be devoted to the poor."

The edndowment, to be administered by seven local trustees, was to provide £60 a year for twenty-one years. The growing desire for better local medical services, of which the Crowfoot endowment was a notable example, was apparent in several Suffolk Jubilee memorials: at Leiston, an isolation wing was added to the hospital, and at Lowestoft, a children's wing.

Dr Crowfoot's letter was reproduced in the local paper, under the heading "A MUNIFICENT GIFT". The suggestion that the town Jubilee memorial should be a house for the Nurse supported by the Crowfoot endowment was, in the circumstances, irresistible; and it eased the Mayor's difficulty by ending public controversy.

5. THE JUBILEE: A PLAN ACCEPTED

A SECOND PUBLIC meeting was promptly called by the Mayor. Again the Town Hall was crowded. The Town Clerk reported on the postcards. "The total number received was 75." (Laughter) – 42 for a Town Hall, 6 for a sanatorium, 24 for almshouses, 2 for nursing staff. One was "Not a Town Hall". (Laughter).

Then the Mayor read Dr Crowfoot's letter. He heartily recommended the proposed endowment and the suggestion that the Beccles Jubilee foundation should be a home for a nurse. He referred to another proposal, received from Miss Field, secretary to the local branch of the British Women's Temperance Association, for the building of a temperance hall to be used for clubs and meetings. "What more fitting," Miss Field wrote, "in which to commemorate a woman's long and noble reign than by helping those who are trying to help and uplift women?"

However, the Jubilee Committee having on the previous evening considered and approved the Crowfoot plan, the Mayor now proposed to the meeting its acceptance. Col.Wilson, seconding, put the cost at £300-£400, in addition to which at least £250 would be needed "for providing the old people with a dinner and the children with a substantial treat."

The proposition was put and carried *nem.con*.

The Mayor then read a letter from Mr A.Pells F.S.I. offering to provide the necessary plans and specifications in carrying out the work, and to superintend the work, both free of charge. (Cheers). Col.Wilson said it had occurred to him that the nurse's home would require to be furnished. He would undertake, with the help of a few gentlemen, to provide the furniture for the house. (Cheers).

Thus the matter was settled. The Town would provide, as its permanent commemoration of the Jubilee, a house for the nurse whose salary would be paid by the Crowfoot endowment in memory of Dr Edward Crowfoot. At the Rector's suggestion, the meeting expressed its appreciation to the Crowfoot family. The singing of a verse of the National Anthem concluded the meeting.

Subscriptions were now invited. The first list, published on April 13th, contained over 120 names. Contributions could be "general" or could specify "for the Nurse's Home" or "for the Rejoicings". The "general" list was headed by:

	£		
The Mayor	25	0	0
Dr W.Aldis Wright	100	0	0
Messrs John Crisp & Son	100	0	0
Messrs William Clowes & Sons	52	10	0
Messrs Elliott & Garrood	30	0	0
Mr W.M.Crowfoot	25	0	0
Messrs Read, Stanford & Gayford	5	5	0

The name of Aldis Wright is found on most Beccles subscription lists. He was the town's most distinguished citizen, resident in Beccles, however, only during Cambridge vacations, for he was Vice-master of Trinity. Second son of George Wright, Baptist minister in Beccles for forty-eight years, Aldis Wright had been educated at the Fauconberge School before proceeding to Cambridge. He was Librarian of Trinity, editor of "the Cambridge Shakespeare" and in 1870 became Secretary to the Old Testament revision company, attending all but one of its 794 meetings between 1870 and 1885. His mastery of Hebrew and long familiarity with English prose of the sixteenth century were ideal qualifications for this task. His contribution to the general Jubilee Fund was typically generous.

On the other list, contributions ranged from £30 to one shilling. A further 80 names appeared the following week, when the total had reached £600— a most auspicious start. Eventually, the

Fund closed at £730, the last contribution, of £5, coming from the Beccles Gas Company.

Even this effort of local co-operation could not bridge the sectarian gulf. A letter of April 27th, suggesting a service in which all denominations should join, was ignored; on Thanksgiving Sunday separate services were held. And the following week this appeared:

Dear Sir,

As Superintendent of the Martyrs' Memorial Sunday School, I had the honour to be invited to attend a meeting of the Diamond Jubilee Treat Committee, on Saturday last, at 7.30 p.m., our worthy Mayor in the chair. I was greatly surprised that a Roman Catholic priest should have the audacity, not only to be on the Committee with *loyal* Protestants, but discussing the arrangements for banners, flags, etc. May we not imagine them, dear sir, flaunting banners of the Pope, followed by others of the Virgin Mary, on their way from the New Market to the Common, halting in front of the Martyrs' Memorial with a hideous grin of satisfaction that Rome's policy was unchanged since the day our noble martyrs were burned? The crimes of that apostate Church cry aloud for vengeance. Shall not we as Protestants listen to the injunction in Rev.xviii, "Come out of her, my people, that ye be not partakers of her sins, and that ye receive not of her plagues." By inserting the above in "The East Suffolk Gazette" you will greatly oblige.

Yours very truly,
A.E.Mount
Superintendent Martyrs' Memorial Sunday School.

It happened that this letter appeared at the time when the religious controversy in the newspaper was at its height — the following week five letters appeared, including, of course, long compositions from "A Suffolk Dissenter" and from

"Vigilans", who made some sarcastic remarks on Mount's letter. But one letter struck a different note, deploring Mount's animosity..."and I must fervently hope, in spite of his letter, we here in Beccles, in celebrating the happy Jubilee of our beloved Sovereign, shall be allowed to forget we are Catholics and Protestants, and remember only that we are Englishmen. *A Burgess of the Borough*."

Meanwhile, the Jubilee Committee proceeded with plans for the Celebration Day, engaging the services of the Artillery Band for £11, the Rifle Band for £10 and the Trumpet Band for £2. Members of Bible classes would be allowed to attend the treat irrespective of age. The Corporation was to be requested "not to allow any booth on the Common for the sale of intoxicating liquors." A bonfire on the Common was to be substituted for the fireworks display previously agreed.

As the great day approached, with arrangements completed, all shared the hope— a fine warm day on June 22nd.

The Jubilee: Small Advertisements

SPECIAL NOTICE: *Now showing, a large stock of National Decorative Cloth. In stripes, Fancies and Plain Colours from 1¾ a yard upwards*

FLAGS

of every description, from 1d to 3/11 each. Medals, Favours, Rosettes, Brooches, Handkerchiefs etc., and many other Novelties from 1d each to 10¾d a doz., suitable for Schools etc.

Large Quantities supplied at Special Prices.

WOMACK BROOKS,

St Andrew's House, Beccles.

6. THE AGE OF EXCURSIONS

OF THE MANY changes in Victoria's reign, none affected rural life more obviously and directly than the coming of the railway. When, in 1853, the first Beccles line was opened, the great event was celebrated by a mammoth dinner to the engineer-promoter Sir Morton Peto—

"A better time is looming in the distance,
Borne onward swift on Peto's golden wing,
Already we behold with Heaven's assistance,
The brightly dawning day he has come to bring...
Welcome, welcome, friend of rich and poor".

By 1897, development was complete: the day of the railway was now at high noon. Becclesians could enjoy shopping in Norwich, an outing to Lowestoft or Yarmouth, or a day in London.

Timetables for the year show, on weekdays—

9 trains to London,	fastest 2 hours 37 minutes
10 trains to Norwich,	fastest 1 hour
11 trains to Yarmouth,	fastest 25 minutes
12 trains to Lowestoft,	fastest 18 minutes

The first London train left at 6.53 a.m., arriving Liverpool Street at 10.30; the last return left at 5 p.m.

It was the Age of Excursions. Those to London were for special events; and the events chosen give a clear indication of the interests of people in a Market Town. The year began with special trains to the Christmas Pantomimes on Tuesdays, January 12th and 26th. The next events, on successive weeks of February and March, were the Horse Shows, at the Agricultural Hall—the Shire Horse Show, the Hackney Horse Show and the Hunter Show (the first two lasted four days each and the last three days).

On the Tuesdays of these three weeks there were excursions from Beccles, the fare 6s return or 7s if you returned the following day. These were the standard excursion charges.

After Horses, Football—an excursion to the Association Cup Final on Saturday April 10th at the Crystal Palace. This was the memorable encounter before a crowd of 65,000 of Aston Villa and Blackburn Rovers, one of the famous finals. But there occurred an unfortunate clash of events, for on this Saturday Beccles Caxton were playing Leiston at Ipswich in the Final of the Suffolk Senior Cup. A tantalising choice for local football fans!

A mere five days later came the Easter holidays excursion, leaving Beccles on a Thursday, to return the following Monday or Tuesday. Other London excursions were:

In May, to the Yachting and Fisheries Exhibition.

In June, to the Handel Festival and to the Diamond Jubilee celebrations, leaving on Monday and returning on Friday.

In July, to the Salvation Army Demonstration (train leaving at 3.05 a.m.)

In August, a Special Train (fare 5s 9d) for the Beccles "Pleasant Sunday Afternoon Society", returning at 11 p.m.

In September, to the Confectioners Exhibition

In October, to the Grocers and Allied Trades Exhibition and to the Dairy Show.

In November, to the Brewers Exhibition and the following week—no special event, but perhaps for Christmas shopping.

In December, to the Cattle Show and on Boxing Day.

It would be misleading to suggest that these excursions were for Beccles only. Trains started from Lowestoft and stopped at several other stations en route to Liverpool Street.

Besides excursions to London, there were others

to Wroxham and Cromer and many to Yarmouth and Lowestoft, at a price even impecunious schoolboys could afford, as A.H.Pye recalled— "I and two chums spent a very happy Bank Holiday at Yarmouth for a total cost of not more than half a crown each. Railway fare was one shilling. Dinner of roast beef, Yorkshire pudding and two veg. followed by a sweet, cost tenpence. A shrimp tea cost 6d." This left one penny for an ice-cream and the last penny on a donkey ride.

The number of people who took advantate of these facilities is indicated by an account of the Saturday P.S.A. trip to London. Over 200 members and others went, some returning the same day, some on Sunday (rail travel on Sunday apparently not objected to), some the following Monday and Wednesday. Of this great day, A.E.Pye recorded: An old man, John Smith, who was over seventy and had never been outside the town before, on arriving at Liverpool Street had been too afraid to venture further; but after waiting there some hours, and beginning to feel thirsty, ventured into Bishopsgate, found a pub and ordered a beer. On the barmaid handing him the drink he remarked, "I expect you'll be funny busy here today miss. There's two hundred on us come up from Beccles." The Caxton Press took a holiday at the same time, their employees having a choice of three outings: to London with the P.S.A. party, a circular river tour via Norwich and Yarmouth, or to Dunwich and Southwold by road. Elliot and Garrod's engineering works closed for the same purpose.

The railway had no road competition in 1897. The motor car was locally unknown. When Fourpawr's circus came to Beccles in May, (the first of three circuses, the others being Fred Ginnett's in August and Sanger's in September), after the list of live attractions: 100 horses, ponies and mules, 300 Birds, Beasts and Reptiles, there was "Another Novelty THE MOTOR CAR, or Horseless Carriage."

A great contrast to these fast and frequent excursion trains is seen in local outings. Annual Sunday School treats were the crown of the children's year. The Church of England Sunday School had between seven and eight hundred scholars. "These young people, accompanied by the Rector, the superintendent and the teachers, with numerous banners and flags flying, would parade through the streets to the castle meadow where the afternoon and evening were spent in games, races, scrambling for sweets and nuts and in sitting on the grass doing justice to a sumptuous tea. The Congregationalists had the next largest Sunday School with 300-350 scholars. They followed the same procedure. And many children managed to escape the strict denominational barrier by attending one school in the morning and another in the afternoon, thus qualifying for two outings! But the really high spot was the Band of Hope outing to Southwold. Early in the morning of the long-awaited day the adults would be up to decorate the miller's wagons which were to convey the party to its destination. These wagons, each drawn by a pair of sturdy carthorses, took three hours to do the twelve miles journey. Shortly after 9 o'clock the children were assembled and packed into the festooned wagons. With excited cheers and shouts they started out upon what to them was a day of adventure. The long, winding country lanes, devoid of all motor traffic, bordered by thickly foliated and untrimmed hedges covered with pale-pink wild roses; the beautiful avenues of massive trees; the scent of the blossoms from the beanfields and new-mown hay; the interchange of meetings from the villagers– these were sources of unspeakable delight. The children certainly were intolerant and intemperate little teetotallers, for they felt it incumbent upon them to boo loudly every public house they passed."[1]

Another outing this year was the Girls Friendly Society's Trip to Fritton Lake. The party numbered 128. On their return, all attended a short service at the Parish Church, followed by the distribution of prizes and cards of merit for four or three years in the same situation. The Railway excursions had made a great change, but the religious organisations still exercised a dominant influence over local outings at which free transport for many children was essential.

1 "Fretwork, Liquorice and the Band of Hope." *East Anglian Magazine*, March 1951.

Humour of the Year

THE SUNDAY SCHOOL EXCURSION: *"Do lend me one of your plaits, Daisy." "No I can't. I want it for myself." "Oh, Daisy! And you got the first prize for unselfishness."*

A CASE *of over-training. — Passing your proper station.*

7. CONTROVERSY OF THE YEAR

THE CONTROVERSY OVER the appointment of a Town Surveyor had caused great acrimony and occupied much space in the local newspaper. There was another controversy which figured even more prominently. It might have been expected that the question of lighting the town— should gas be replaced by electricity?— would have been debated, as something of great local importance. But the dispute was quite different; it was the Roman Catholics versus the Dissenters. Non-conformity, long-established, flourished in Beccles. The Roman Catholics had recently built their large church; and when, under the zealous and energetic Father Meinrad Fulton, they established "St Catherine's Convent", it was not surprising that Nonconformists showed voluble alarm, especially as the claims of the Roman church were vigorously assisted in a series of lectures in the town: "Why I joined the Church of Rome", "Why I believe in an Infallible Pope", and "Why I go to Confession", by Lister Drummond. Throughout the year, letters of tedious length, strong animus and variable scholarship occupied numerous columns in the local newspaper. Now and then the Editor entered, in vain, a brief protest.

The first issue of the year contained the first of many letters from "A Suffolk Dissenter" under the heading "The Question of Persecution". His main contentions were that the Roman Catholics had always practiced persecution and that their aim was to destroy religious freedom. "I know that nuns will go about with sweet smiles and appeals to be 'charitable' etc. etc., but it should strictly be borne in mind that the concealed object of their whole work is to set up *a political despotism under the cloak of religion*."

After a relatively brief skirmish on the question: "Was Luther responsible for the Seven

Years War?" the Catholic "Vigilans" entered the lists with a long epistle on "Luther and his Spiritual Descendants" in which he made great play with the alleged scandalous behaviour of the Protestant missionaries in Tahiti. "Rev Mr — attached himself not to one, but actually to *two* Tahitian females, and with one of them he continued to cohabit until he quitted the isle ... I wonder, Mr Editor, whether Rev Mr — was a Suffolk Dissenter? I should not be at all surprised if such were the true, actual fact."

"A Suffolk Dissenter" and "Vigilans" continued to plough these bitter furrows for several weeks in letters up to 1,400 words long. Before February was out, "A Disliker of Rant" had entered the controversy in support of "Vigilans"; and the Editor added: "We have in hand another letter from "Suffolk Dissenter" which must close this correspondence."

"Suffolk Dissenter", however, soon had another opponent and another theme— "Sacerdotalism". An Anglo-Catholic having taken exception to some asides in one of "S.D's" previous letters, he devoted another letter to the contention: "Sacerdotalism leads straight to Rome."

In March, a short letter announced that St Catherine's Convent had been opened one afternoon for all who wished to see over it— "Beccles will shortly be recognised as a very important centre of Catholicity." Predictably, "Suffolk Dissenter" was provoked! He called on all Protestants "to imitate the zeal of their Roman and Ritualist rivals," citing Dickens' comments on Convents and Confessionals in Ireland and on the Continent as leading to "social and political degradation". He raised again the issue of persecution by Rome— and this brought "Vigilans" into action to assert that Protestant missionaries were often persecutors. "Vigilans" ended thus: "Not many of your Christian sects can boast of their freedom from the taint of persecution, excepting the Society of Friends and the Salvation Army. One can admire the latter at a respectable distance, and wish its members success, provided they carry out their proposed plan of raising from misery those unhappy people that are swallowed up among the submerged tenth."

At the same time— we have reached the end of April— "A German Catholic" joined in, and "Suffolk Dissenter" received a rap from an unexpected quarter:

> "If "Suffolk Dissenter", as a schoolboy, had sent up themes so stupid and overloaded with useless quotations as are his letters to "East Suffolk Gazette", he would have been spanked.
>
> Yours faithfully,
>
> SCHOOL-BOY."

Neither "Suffolk Dissenter" not his opponents took the slightest notice of this and several issues in May had two full columns of controversial letters, of increasingly bitter tone, including that of A.E.Mount quoted in another chapter, and the long-suffering Editor intervened again— "We have several further letters on these subjects from "A German Catholic", A.E.Mount and other correspondents, but the correspondence is now closed."

But not for long! The excitement of the Jubilee over, battle re-commenced. Father Fulton and John Flower, son of the former Beccles Congregational minister, joined the fray. Flower's long letter of mid-July, on "The Adoration of the Pope", brought another editorial "Having devoted considerable space to this and other controversies affecting the Roman Catholics, and exhausted, we fear, the patience of many of our readers, our columns must now be closed to letters on these subjects."

The meeting at Barsham of the Beccles and Lowestoft Branch of the English Church Union at the end of August, attended by eighty members, considered "The practical conditions necessary for re-union between the Orthodox Eastern Church and the Anglican Church." This led to further controversy. Father Fulton's "Remarks on the Meeting at Barsham" ridiculed the idea of re-union, because the Anglican Church had no settled doctrine: "What is the teaching authority in the Church of England? Anybody may believe anything he likes and yet remain a Churchman." A long reply came from "Oriens", in which the writer concentrated upon "the outrageous claims of many Papal Bulls— These pretensions, which at the close of the nineteenth century, provoke nothing but a smile, had a different effect at the close of the sixteenth; for they led to the Spanish Armada. The ideas contained in them are now dormant but do they not still exist?" However, this correspondence required no editorial intervention and petered out, in relative amity, at the end of October.

In November religious conflict entered another local field. It was time for the election of a new Mayor and Councillor Banham was a probable candidate. Now Banham, a builder who had helped Beccles with its useful Bathing-Place, was a Roman Catholic. Efforts were made to persuade Alderman Rix to become Mayor, a special private meeting of the Council being held. It was clear that a move was on foot to prevent the election of a Roman Catholic. Rix declined. At once a more determined effort was made to get Alderman Wilson to accept the office, the Deputy-Mayor leading a deputation. But Wilson also declined. Then came the Quarterly Meeting of the Council on Nov.9th— the occasion marked by a free Supplement in the next issue of the local paper— and when the retiring Mayor asked for a nomination, and Councillor Banham was proposed and seconded, only four hands were raised in his support. "On the Mayor noting the number, a fifth hand was raised for the proposition." That was just sufficient. Beccles had its first Roman Catholic Mayor.

Next Sunday the new Mayor attended Mass wearing his official robes. Special seats in front of the altar had been prepared for him and the Mayoress; and gratification at the election of a co-religionist was expressed in the sermon. This letter followed:

The Mayoralty of Beccles

Sir,

What is the meaning, if any, of the very odd talk, indulged in at the dinner to the retiring Mayor, paid to the co-religionists of our newly-elected Chief Magistrate? What on earth has his election to do with his religious opinions? Is our public dinner table to become a field for the spread of Roman Catholic propaganda? I do not remember that, when an English Catholic has been elected to this high office, Churchmen have expressed their gratitude, or that the election of a Baptist or an Independent has called forth such expressions from the leading members of those religious bodies. Papists, who take it as a compliment that their friend and fellow-worshipper is elected Mayor of Beccles, seem strangely given to laying flattering unction to their souls.

I am, sir, yours faithfully,
EARNEST ENQUIRER

This was the final shot of the year. But the conflict was not confined to those who could put a lengthy pen to paper. At Beccles Police Court in November, Robert Smith was charged with assaulting an elderly widow named Sarah Reeder; and it transpired that the case arose out of the ill-feeling in the neighbourhood because defendant and his family were Roman Catholics. Smith was found guilty and fined £1.

8. THE NEW ATHLETICISM

BECCLES COULD BOAST an outstanding marksman, Sergeant Harry Tilney of the Artillery Volunteers. This was not his best year at Bisley, but elsewhere he did well, winning cups and prizes in several competitions. At Yarmouth in May he achieved a splendid 101 out of a possible 105; and his successes always made news. For in 1897 sport occupied far more space in newspapers than it had done a few years earlier. More people played games; more were interested in the results. Cycling and athletics had achieved recent prominence; cricket and football had increased in popularity. Tennis now had its place. Swimming was encouraged in boys' schools. This review of the sporting year may begin with the obvious point: sport had a large part in local life.

The Suffolk Senior Football Cup was the most important local competition. Beccles Caxton had won the Cup in 1891-92 and reached the final in 1895-96, when Ipswich Town beat them 2-0. They had reached the final again in Jubilee year, when, on April 9th, they played Leiston at Portman Road. The local paper devoted a full column to the game, which Caxton won 1-0, and another half-column to the welcome home and the immediate celebration of victory. The winners arrived at Beccles Station at 8.30 p.m. to find awaiting them a large cheering crowd and the inevitable band. A long procession of torchbearers escorted them through the streets and a celebration with champagne and songs followed at the King's Head.

There were troubles, however, in the local football world. Allegations that some clubs practised clandestine professionalism were proved well founded, when Kirkley were disqualified from the Amateur Cup for having played a man who had been a professional and had not been re-instated as an amateur. There were other rumours of payments to players supposedly amateurs. And rough play was rampant. Lowestoft were among the worst offenders. In their game against Caxton two players were cautioned for deliberately kicking opponents. The following week, against Beccles Town, as a Beccles man was going through with the ball, a Lowestoft player shouted— so the local paper, with uncharacteristic forthrightness, reported— "Kick him in the ------!"

Beccles spectators could be vociferously partisan too. When in Caxton's match against King's Lynn the referee awarded a corner against the home team, he was jeered by the crowd "and found it necessary to caution some of the spectators". There was more trouble after the match, leading the local reporter to comment: "really, this sort of thing won't do, you know. Spectators *must* learn to control their feelings...."

Including both 1st and 2nd elevens of Beccles Caxton, Beccles Town, the College and Fauconberge, there were at least a dozen teams playing regularly at this time, besides the youngsters— Caxton Juniors, College Day Boys, Choir Boys, and others— who competed in the "Beccles Junior Shield Competition".

Thus football was exceedingly popular, and cricket was little less so. The Fauconberge School, whose Headmaster had formerly played for Kent, had the strongest cricket team, but Beccles College gained the highest reflected glory of the season when its former pupil, G.L.Jessup, scored a hurricane 42 in a quarter of an hour to see Cambridge on the way to an easy win over Oxford. Many rural clergymen played cricket. Two or three would often turn out for Benacre Park, including the former Blue, Rev T.S.Curteis, of whom F.C. Oakley gave this account: "He was extremely irascible, and after having been given out lbw would return to the pavilion purple in the face, calling upon high heaven to witness that not only was his leg not in front of the wicket, but that the ball never touched it. We schoolboys were delighted to note that he was rubbing his leg as he made this protest."

The standard of cricket of the private schools was much higher than that of any other local sides, and their strongest opponents were other schools like Framlingham and Ipswich. Beccles Caxton had two teams and Elliott and Garrood's works fielded a side occasionally. Cricket does not seem to have been played much in the surrounding villages, where pub-based quoits was far more popular.

Tennis was growing in popularity. The Beccles Club (subscriptions: Gentlemen 10s, Ladies 7/6, Family Tickets one guinea) began the season with thirty members, several more joining during the season—"the secretary begins to hope that Beccles people are at last beginning to see that Lawn Tennis is not always a game of 'pat-ball'." Most matches were for mixed teams, but some were for ladies only. When a ladies team from Yarmouth came over, it was thought worthy of mention that "Miss English's overhand service was very effective".

Archery was no longer popular and hockey for girls a distant prospect. The only sport besides tennis—and croquet on private lawns—in which ladies took an occasional part was rowing. At the Regatta in July there was "A Rowing Race for Ladies". But that was the only feminine event in a long programme of Sailing Races with all-male crews and Aquatic sports, among which were four swimming races (one for boys), a Shovel Race, a Polo Match and the popular "Walking the Greasy Pole".

The river provided the townspeople with plenty of sport. Beccles College had its own Swimming Sports with fifteen events. The boys of the Fauconberge School had an early swim on fine summer mornings. They were awakened by the Porter who walked into the dormitory ringing a handbell and proclaiming: "Five and twenty to seven, gentlemen! Bathing: sixty-eight." The figure gave the temperature of the water: if it was below fifty, there was no bathing that morning. There was good fishing, too, in the Waveney. Among letters this year in "Answers", dealing with the question "WHERE SHALL WE GO?" (for a holiday), was this:

> My choice is the quiet little town of Beccles, with a population of six or seven thousand, just large enough to get creature comforts without the annoyance of having to wait for the carrier or next London parcel, as in some out-of-the-way holiday resorts. There the cyclist, angler, yachtsman, photographer or botanist may find ample occupation and objects of interest.
>
> Lodgings are cheap, clean and plentiful; the town having a large income from the marshes, the inhabitants are very lightly rated. Easy access by train or road to the seaside or the lovely Norfolk Broads. Boating and Fishing on the Waveney— good rowing-boats fourpence per hour; sailing yachts at proportionate prices, according to size; good roads for cycling; old-world scenery for photographers and artists. What more can one desire?
>
> It can be reached from London (109 miles) by a 15s return ticket, and a month's sojourn need not cost above £5 or £6, according to the taste of the individual.

But perhaps the most popular of all the sporting activities was Athletics. Special trains were arranged to Beccles for the seventeenth annual meeting of the Caxton Athletic Club. The Recreation Ground had a track suitable for cycling as well as for running. Competitors came from King's Lynn, Yarmouth, Norwich, Thetford, Ipswich and other East Anglian towns. There were no events for women.

1. *Main Schoolroom at the Fauconberge School in the 1890's*
(From a photograph in the possession of H. R. Hadingham Esq.)

2. *Sergeant Harry Tilney*, 2nd Battalion Norfolk Regt. and 5th Suffolk Regt. Winner of 'The Daily Graphic' International Camp 1902. Five times a finalist in 'The King's 100'.

Indeed, the new athleticism, in a socially conservative town like Beccles, had made little impact on women's lives. And the part played by women in public affairs remained negligible. Mrs Rowsell, the Rector's wife, was secretary of the local branch of the R.S.P.C.A.; there were two ladies on the Committee of the Choral Society; the Domestic Committee of the Hospital consisted of four ladies; the National School had a Ladies Committee— as had the Tennis Club. There were charitable organisations run by ladies, such as the Dorcas Society and the Womens' Temperance Scoiety. But on none of the following were women represented: the main Hospital Committee; the Burial Board; the Public Library; the Literary Institute; the P.S.A. Society; the Floricultural Society; the Regatta Committee. At the public meetings to discuss what form the permanent Jubilee memorial should take, not one woman spoke.

Humour of the Year

THE FRENCHMAN'S FIRST MATCH: *"Vot for dey make all de shout?" "Because a goal was taken." - "And ees id because of all de noise dat you call it de game de foot bawl?"*

AT THE MATCH: *Curate (to young lady of fifteen): "Isn't Tom Jones's fielding splendid!" Her mother (indignantly): "Sir! My daughter has never been allowed to read* that *class of literature."*

"WHAT *beautiful hands Miss Brownjohn has got! I wonder what she does to get them like that?" "Nothing at all."*

9. "MR MACADAM" LITERARY CYCLIST

SHORTLY AFTER JAMES Hissey had started, in a dog-cart, the tour he was to describe in *Over Fen and Wold* (1889) he came across the following notice, appended to an old inn sign:

Good Accommodation
and
Stabling
for
Cyclists and Motorists.

Further on, at the little town of Falkingham, (the railway had not reached it) he saw on a church porch:

Cyclists Welcomed
In Cycling Dress.

A holiday on the Broads might include cycling excursions. Anne Dodd tells how, when sailing from Yarmouth in a wherry, she met a friend sailing in the opposite direction, who had left her companions at Horning— "taking a spin on their wheels; we've four bicycles on board". (*On the Broads*, 1896). A writer in *The Nineteenth Century and After* asserted that cycling as a fashionable craze was played out, but "for country visiting, when carriages are not available, cycles will always hold their own; especially as the long-talked of motor-car seems likely to end in smoke— and a bad smell."

Cycling had made its impression upon rural life during the '80s; but a far greater impact was felt in the '90s. "Cycling during the last two or three years has lifted all classes of society into the saddle" according to the review of "The Record Reign" in *The East Suffolk Gazette*.

Beccles in 1897 was a centre of cycling activity. In Station Road, at the temperance commercial hotel, Miss Dora Saul offered accommodation particularly for cyclists, whilst Mr Fred Smith at his coffee tavern advertised "teas and dinners provided, parties catered for, every accommodation for bicyclists." Also in Station Road was Robinson's Cycle Depot which stocked all the leading makes except Raleigh's and offered "machines on hire". In late January, Robinson started the commercial cycling season with a two-day Exhibition in the Town Hall, specially decorated for the occasion; some thirty or more cycles of the newest pattern were displayed on a raised platform. There was also a large display of accessories. One of the purchasers of a cycle was the Mayor of Beccles. "Instrumental music was provided at intervals by Miss Wellswood." Three weeks later, the other Beccles supplier, Mr G.C.Field, had his exhibition in the Corn Hall (originally Fisher's Theatre), decorated by a local draper, W.F.Spaull.

Both these exhibitions were appraised by "Mr MacAdam", pseudonym of *The East Suffolk Gazette* correspondent whose Cycling Notes— often a full column— appeared at regular intervals during the season. MacAdam was a lively and knowledgeable critic. After praising the machines he judged good — "The Ladies No.2 Raleigh struck me as quite the best thing in the exhibition"— he launched a heavy attack on misleading salesmanship: "A comparatively new make is the Valkyrie. My attention was particularly called to the barrel hub fitted to this make. It appeared to me good of its kind, and ingeniously constructed, but when an attendant informed me that barrel hubs of this pattern were fifteen yards in the mile better than any cup or cone hub— well, then I laughed! ... A barrel hub worth fifteen yards in the mile— ridiculous nonsense! The hub may well be all right— and on the other hand may be a nuisance— but to claim impossible advantages for it is merely silly."

MacAdam had much useful advice of offer. On April 6 he wrote: "All you who think of selling your old machines, now is the time to set about it, just before Easter machines sell like hot cakes.

The other day I had three enquiries for one before it had been advertised four and twenty hours."

On May 11 he castigated the "sixpenny-an-hour brigade" who showed reckless disregard for the rules of the road. "All cyclists, young or old, should remember that by not keeping to their proper side in passing, overtaking, or being passed, they not only risk their own necks and machines, but those of other people as well. Moreover, in case of an accident, the party in fault would be held liable to pecuniary damages, which might be rather heavy. It is just as well to remember these things." And coverage was available in Beccles from F.E.Miles of Station Road– "Why not insure you cycle against Accident, Fire and Theft? Premiums from 7s 6d including £100 FATAL ACCIDENT POLICY."

There were two men's cycling clubs in the town, the Caxton Club and the newly-formed Beccles Athletic Club, which also organised athletics, cricket and football. The club cycling began towards the end of May. Both clubs went to Yarmouth for their first run. MacAdam included a sarcastic note on one of these: "The Town Club had a very fair muster for its opening run on Wednesday. Some of the members found half-way quite far enough. Really energetic! I should recommend a motor car."

There was some mixed cycling. Lady members of Bungay A.C. were invited to join an evening run to Harleston, "six ladies and eleven 'diamond frames' taking part, the other machine being a tandem. Rain threatened all the evening, and although it spoiled the attendance, the comfort of the freedom from dusty roads made every one forgiving. Altogether, the run was voted a decided success." A Ladies cycling club named "The Southwold Wheelers" had just been formed; and in July the "Gentlemen's Club of Southwold" invited these Ladies to a picnic on Walberswick Common. Some social pleasure was often an object of cycle clubs' outings– as when the Caxton club cycled, in late June, to Hedenham Memorial, where tea and strawberries ad lib. were served.

Several cycling races were included in the Caxton Athletic Sports in July. An entrance fee of 2s a race was charged and the first Prizes were worth £3 10s. To "MacAdam's" chagrin, competitors from outside the town won the open events.

The highlight of the cycling year, on July 31st, was the run to London of some members of the Athletic Club, "MacAdam" himself being one. Twenty members and friends mustered to cheer the intrepid party— for a cycle ride to London was no easy undertaking— as it set off from the King's Head at 11.30 p.m. A break of ten minutes was made at Saxmundham for coffee, stewed fruit and light refreshments. "Fortunately," wrote MacAdam in his account the following week, "the road was by no means bad after leaving Saxmundham. I cannot say so much of the road from Beccles to Blythburgh, which was quite disgraceful. Where is the County Council and where are the local Councillors?"

At this point the party consisted of eleven, but only seven completed the long ride. Punctures occurred with increasing frequency as the party approached London. "The night was dark as pitch and afforded a good test for lamps. At times we had to ride by instinct and trust that the inky blackness contained no hidden danger. Once we came across a cart in the middle of a downward slope. With great courtesy, the owner— I wish I knew his name, so as to be able to send him the club's thanks— had pulled up on the left side, and sent his groom to the horse's head. Only this, and his kindly warning 'Keep to the left!' saved us from what would, at the best, have been a very narrow shave."

Nine cyclists reached Stratford Bridge, where a light breakfast had been arranged— "but by some mischance our letter was sent unstamped, and the landlady had refused to take it in, unmindful of the fact that the bill for our breakfast would have, at least, repaid the necessary two pence and perhaps left a profit! 'The Gun Inn' is where we hoped for our much-wanted light breakfast. We did not get it. The 'Gun Inn' is 'off'." But they got their breakfast, and a good wash, at Chelmsford; and there the photographers of the party took some snaps. On they went to Ongar and Chigwell, delayed by punctures—"While the Portable Repairer struggled with tyres gaspingly, and the rest of us slept the sleep of the tired cyclist. However, at length we found ourselves fairly in the smoke, and the six miles of bumpy macadam became gradually less and less, till at last we were in the City and the journey over. So ended our first club run to London."

"MacAdam" was fond of including light verse in his Notes. The best of the year, by Fred Gillett, was:

Ow'd Charlie a-larnin'

We wonderful laughed
  At ow'd partner Charlie,
As we set on the shaft
  Of a wagon o'barley.
    We'd had fourses,
    Unyooked the hosses,
  And stopped worruk right 'arly,
  When, behow'd ye, come Charlie!
We wonderful laughed!

We wonderful smiled,
  He was then a-tarnin'
The corner o' the fe'ld,
  Says he, "I'm a-larnin'
    This here new invention—"
    That worn't his intention,
  But, behow'd ye, he sorter
  Downed, like a tippen-a-torter,

Inter a deek full o'water.
Oover goo Charlie!
We wonderful smiled!

He was wonderful wild
When he slubbed out and shivered;
His dopper was sp'iled,
And with muck he was kivvered.
But he doon'd trouble!
Up he mount like a bubble,
Gooin' wiggly-warly, wiggly-warly!
"Up again!" say ow'd Charlie;
And, trewly to tarl ye,
He bumped inter the shaft
As if he was daft,
And his wheels come in halft—
We wonderful laughed!

And I'd give an arternoon's
Wages, and my ow'd bewts,
For one o' them camerooms
(For takin' o' snap-shewts)
To ha' took his footygraft!
Yow'd ha' wonderful laughed!

Another use for cycles was demonstrated this year when a man from a neighbouring village pedalled in to give the alarm for a small fire. The Church bells were jangled, the Brigade assembled— and was in time to prevent serious damage.

Humour of the Year

WHAT KEEPS THEM AWAY: *Maud: "What makes Clara go to church every Sunday?" Martha: "Because she hasn't got a bicycle."*

OVER THE TEA-CUPS: *"So the dear Bishop has taken to bicycling?" "Yes, they call him the sermon on the mount."*

10. THE JUBILEE: OCCASION FOR COMPLACENCY

THE SPECIAL JUBILEE Number of *The East Suffolk Gazette*, besides a double page inset with photographs of incidents of the reign, of the Royal residences and, in the centre, of the Queen and the Royal Family, printed a full-page review of "The Record Reign". It was predictably, with ample justification but extreme complacency, a record of Progress— "the steady advances which have increased a hundredfold the sum of national happiness, national intelligence and national morality." The contrast between Past and Present was driven home: "When the Queen was called to reign ... the masses of the people led a hard, cheerless life of grinding poverty, unable for the most part to read or write and with scarcely any voice in the government of the country. Trade was hampered by protective tariffs, the price of bread was high, the criminal law was savage and ferocious and the Poor Laws were harsh and cruel."

The "General Retrospect" was followed by accounts of:

1. The Expansion of the Empire: "the most wonderful and powerful empire the world has ever seen." "... it is remarkable that attempts to throw off the British control are so few in number. The explanation is that the yoke is light, and that Englishmen have a genius for governing the races that are subject to them."

2. The Colonies: "The British Colonial system is now the pride of every Englishman and the envy of our foreign rivals."

3. The Progess of Science: "the field is so wide and the discoveries so manifold and marvellous that the most we can attempt to do is to indicate a few of the directions in which the age has moved forward."

"Steam has annihilated distance."

3. *Celebration of the Diamond Jubilee*. The triple archway before the entrance to Beccles Station. (From a photograph in the possession of F. Denson Esq., Beccles Borough Archivist)..

"Next to steam we have to thank electricity for the most marvellous progress that the age has made... In 1873 it took six months before news of an event in Australia could reach London. Now, before four minutes have elapsed,they know in the streets of Sydney the winner of the English Derby or the result of the University Boat Race..."

"The telephone helps still further to annihilate distance. The electric light turns night into day."

"No one can write or speak without the greatest satisfaction of the progress which has been made in the great science of medicine and the art of healing. Who can measure the agony which the human race has been spared through the one discovery of the use of anaesthetics?"

"Bacteriology is a science of the last few years, which has already worked marvels, and has still greater wonders in store."

4. Industrial Progress: "the marvellous rapidity with which invention has succeeded...invention in almost every part of industry."

"We consumed in 1837, 406,000,000 lb. of cotton; in 1895 we consumed more than 1,400,000,000 lb.; our output of coal is thirty-four times as great as it was, our shipping has risen 700 per cent, our foreign trade has risen 450 per cent."

"Few industries have grown in such a markedly rapid fashion as the tobacco and cycle trades ...the Chancellor of the Exchequer stated last year that a quarter of a million sterling is wasted annually in cigarette ends."

"There are, of course, spots on the sun of prosperity. The problem of the unemployed still remains to be solved and keeps appearing every winter in a more or less acute form."

"A second great difficulty is the rapid depopulation of the country districts. That has been an inevitable, but still a deplorable result of the agricultural depression, ...yet the conditions of the agricultural labourer's life are far more happy than they were in the days before the abolition of the Poor Laws...his cottage is a palace compared with what it was sixty years ago."

5. Manners and Customs: "In many respects we are undoubtedly better than our fathers. We no longer fight duels as points of honour. We drink less. Intoxication is now a serious breach of social decorum."

"One of the great social changes has been what we may conveniently describe as the woman movement."

"National sports have become far less cruel than they were. The national conscience has become more tender. The cock-fights, the badger-drawings, the bull-baitings that delighted our great grandfathers are now things of the past; the prize ring has been abolished; cruelty to animals is punished."

"If we look at the sports of the masses, we find cricket and football supreme. Cricket has spread to all ends of the earth. The supremacy of football throughout eight months of the year is even more striking. Cycling in the last two or three years has become very popular."

"The passion for athletics is universal at the present day. In the leading schools of the country and at the universities success at games is esteemed almost as highly as success in the class lists and there are many who consider that athletics now occupy too prominent a place in the educational system of the land."

"We have seen a sturdy growth of the humanitarian spirit during the era...hospitals have sprung up on every side, and all forms of charitable institutions flourish and multiply."

"A striking change has come over the character of such an apparently settled institution as the English Sunday. The old narrow Sabbatarian notions have disappeared...Sunday has become a holiday, as well as a holy day, to the great masses of population."

"Another great change has been the holiday movement...owing to the increased facilities for travelling and the cheap trains provided during the summer, the very poorest in the land are not debarred from a holiday at the seaside."

6. The Victorian Age of Literature: "...a host of illustrious names that will make the nineteenth century famous in the literary annals of the world."

"No account would be complete without some reference to the remarkable growth of journalism ...the daily newspaper now finds its way into almost every household in the land."

Similar enthusiastic accounts of the great reign appeared in other local newspapers. *The Ipswich Journal* selected for special mention these two aspects– "the steady and peaceful advance of democracy...everyone eats better food and more of it." The general complacency found a sober and dignified expression in the concluding prayer of the authorised Thanksgiving Service: "O Lord our heavenly Father, we give Thee hearty thanks for the many blessings Thou hast bestowed on us during the sixty years of the happy reign of our gracious Queen Victoria. We thank Thee for progress made in the knowledge of Thy marvellous works, for increase of comfort given to human life, for kindlier feeling between rich and poor, for wonderful preaching of Thy gospel to many nations..."

11. THE JUBILEE: DAY OF CELEBRATION

A HOT DRY summer had followed the spring floods. Dust accumulated in the town, so that at the end of May a correspondent wrote:

STREET WATERING

Dear Sirs,

Can you kindly inform me if the street-watering is partly abandoned, as during the past week the dust has flown to such an extent that really my time is thrown away in summer cleaning. I made enquiries as to the Corporation water-carts, and found that the painting is completed (generally done when they should be watering the streets); but on Saturday morning, after cleaning my eyes from dust, I started in search to see whether they could be found, and on my way to the Common discovered one on the Nurseries meadow, watering grass. I think, Sir, that first our streets should be attended to, and after that is done no one would object to a tip to our poorly paid Corporation employees. Will our surveyor kindly look to this or he will hear further from,

Yours truly

A Summer Cleaner.

A rejoinder in *The Beccles Record* the following week suggested, however, that "A Summer Cleaner" merely wanted to have a nasty little dig at the Surveyor!

Some rain fell on Thanksgiving Sunday, when the Mayor and Corporation heard the rector preach on the universal theme of the day, and the Nonconformists held a united service at which the preacher remarked: "One thing stands out prominent above all others with us, and that is the spread of the Gospel during the past sixty years."

But Tuesday June 22nd, the Day of Celebration, was fine and hot. The town was gay with bunting, flags and all sorts of decorations, including a triumphal arch of evergreens and African grasses in Station Road with "God bless the Queen" over the main arch and "1837-1897" over the smaller ones on each side. The only hitch was at the Town Hall, where an accident with the halliards prevented the hoisting of the Union Jack.

Official proceedings began with a special meeting of the Town Council, when the Mayor proposed the adoption of an address of congratulation to the Queen, which ended: "It is our heartfelt prayer...that your descendants may follow your Majesty's bright example and sit upon the throne of this great empire for centuries to come."

The Mayor and his daughter distributed fruit and flowers at the hospital before the next item in the programme— the luncheon at the King's Head at 11.30 a.m. for the Corporation and other privileged persons, an all-male affair. There being a tight schedule for the day, speeches were briefer than they would otherwise have been. The Queen's health was drunk in bumpers of champagne. The Mayor had yet another speech to deliver at the next event— the dinner at the Town Hall for three hundred old people.

"I am speaking," he said, "to some who are able to look back not only on the Coronation of our good Queen, but also on the Coronations of William IV and George IV. You would all agree that never in your memories have things been better than they are today"— cheers— "never were the privileges and the social and domestic comforts equal to those we enjoy at the present time." The Artillery Band stationed in front of the Hall played selections during the dinner, which concluded, of course, with the National Anthem.

At half past one the children of the Board and National schools assembled at their respective buildings, the Artillery Band leading the former and the Rifle Band the latter, to the New Market, where a Jubilee hymn was followed by the inevitable Anthem, three cheers for the Queen and one for the Mayor.

One School, the Fauconberge Grammar, did not join in to the full. It seems that, even on this day of national unity, a barrier of social exclusiveness remained. A writer in *The Ipswich Journal* remarked upon something rather similar in the county town in his description of the assembled children: "It was a glorious and soul stirring sight. It did one's heart good to hear their merry shouts and to see the salutes, military and otherwise (mostly otherwise) with which they acknowledged the Mayor as they passed him. All but one school, and they went by in solemn silence. As I stood behind the Mayor, someone whispered 'Not a sound was heard!' evidently thinking of 'The Burial of Sir John Moore':

'Not a sound was heard, not a jubilant note,
As their feet o'er the gravel they hurried;
Not a scholar discharged a Jubilee shout,
They might as well all have been buried.'

Oh caste, caste, caste! On a day like this at least all distinctions should have been buried. I picked up these lines in the Park next morning; I wondered if they referred to this point:

'We are, we are, we are
So very su-pe-ri-or;
We don't make a noise,
Like rude little boys,
We're so su-pe-ri-or'

But to return to Beccles New Market— where, the cheering over, the Mayor now headed the long procession to the Common. Flags and banners waved. In the crowd was a venerable old lady of 99, in her wheel-chair, watching as the children, gleeful and excited, each waving a rosette and medal portrait of the Queen, shouted lustily; and the hot sun shone gaily as the columns marched to the Common. There, after games, tea was brewed in large coppers and served to 2,000 children. Then there were races and competitions for 500 small prizes. Meanwhile, for older children and adults, a programme of sports was held in which events of contemporary interest were added to some of the old favourites of traditional Rural Sports: the coarse and rougher delights of Grinning through a Halter or Chasing a Pig with a greasy tail were no longer acceptable. Events included: One Mile and Two Miles Bicycle Handicaps; 200 yards, quarter mile and one mile races; Hop, Leap and Jump; Egg and Spoon Race; Wheelbarrow, Sack and Donkey Races (one donkey refused to start); and an Obstacle Race, in which competitors had to colour their faces, climb under and over scaffold poles and through tubs, and to mount a cross-pole fifteen feet high, and there toast the Queen— with lemonade! These strenuous excitements lasted from three until nearly seven. As dusk approached, the Avenue leading from the town to the Common was lit by tiny coloured lamps on the trees. Rockets were discharged from the Church Tower and burst in scintillating colours far overhead to the wonder and delight of the children.

Soon after nine, a procession of cyclists emerged to parade through the streets, in varied and colourful array, the ladies much in evidence— Mrs L.Bloomfield as "Union Jack" (and very comely too), Miss E.Bloomfield attractively dressed as "Maypole Soap", two dainty "girls in blue", whilst a lad named Riches as "Queen Victoria" enjoyed himself in graciously acknowledging the loyal greetings from the thronged streets. And so to the bonfire, on the highest point of the Common, fired at five past ten. It burned for three hours. Thus ended the "official programme".

Some larger places arranged events of greater novelty like the cricket match at Lakenham in Norwich, where teams dressed as Victorian worthies played a closely contested game. "The Duke of

Wellington", "Disraeli", and, alas, "W.G.Grace" all made ducks, but "John Bull" was an appropriate top scorer.

At Gorleston, the mammoth bonfire on the beach, supported by scaffold poles laced with wire, and primed by barrels of tar and lashings of oil, made a fantastic spectacle. But the Beccles celebrations were well worthy of a small town, and had a happy impromptu ending, when, about midnight, a popular publican was moved to "ring the changes" on his concertina. He began in an empty Market Place, but a crowd collected to join him in the National Anthem, which rang through the stillness to bring a vociferous end to the day's patriotic rejoicings. The services of the police had not been required.

A treat for the infants (aged 3-5) was held the following afternoon: they were taken in waggons to the Common for games and tea. Finally, on Thursday evening, the Mayoress gave to children of the National and Board schools copies of the Rev C. Bullock's book *The Queen's Resolve*.

Humour of the Year

JUBILEE ADVERTISEMENT: *Procession— opportunity to view— A few excellent seats to view her Majesty's progress to St Paul's Cathedral are still to be had on the chimney-pots of a nobleman's mansion, commanding a very fine view of one of the leading thoroughfares. Price ten guineas a seat, except for that on the kitchen chimney, for which, as there will necessarily be a lighted fire below, only six guineas will be charged. Early application is absolutely necessary to secure places. Address: Lord ..., Piccadilly, W.*

12. A POLICEMAN'S LOT WAS NOT A PEACEFUL ONE

BECCLES POLICE COURT, Friday January 1st. Herbert Davy, fisherman, Beccles, pleaded guilty to using obscene language to his brother in the Score on December 5th. P.C.Lusher proved the case and said the defendant used very foul language to his brother who was convicted at the previous court. Fined 5s.; thirteen days allowed to pay.

William Drew, labourer, Beccles, was charged with being drunk and disorderly on the 23rd December in Ballygate Street. P.C.Leftly said the defendant was very drunk and shouted and swore at the top of his voice. When told to go away, he said he "could do" two or three policemen. Fined 10s.; or 7 days in default...

"Drunk and disorderly" was a charge frequently preferred at Beccles Police Court, and "obscene language" frequently aggravated the offence. A letter in *The Lowestoft Journal* the week after a foul-mouthed female had been goaled for a fortnight illustrates the sensitivity of late Victorian ears to swearing:

THE LANGUAGE OF OUR STREETS

"...at present, the language used in our streets by mere boys and girls is very bad indeed and the suggestive actions and obscene expression of dissolute women simply shocking. This needs to be put down with a strong hand."

The policeman's job of arresting the truculent drunkard was all in an evening's work— especially a Saturday evening! Truncheons were carried. Sometimes they had to be used.

The town was full of public houses. Several publicans supplemented their income by a second job. John Cracknell at the Angel was a marine store dealer; Will Barber at the Bear and Bells and Tom Strowger at the Fleece were horse-breakers; Luke Smith at the Duke had a porkbutcher's business; Fred Hall at the Falcon made scrape cake, cart grease, neatsfoot oil and engine tallow; Arthur Warren was a blacksmith as well as a beer-retailer; and George Fenn at the Crown was a rat-catcher.

It was outside the Crown that an unruly crowd had assembled at 11.15 p.m. on Saturday May 15th. The Crown was in Blyburgate; there were three other public houses quite near. P.C.Lusher was on duty there. Among the crowd were Alfred and John Caston, labourers, and Samuel Roofe, dealer. Alfred Caston swore at Lusher as he approached; and when told to go home quietly, followed the constable down the road shouting abuse. Lusher repeated his warning. On this Caston peeled off his jacket spoiling for a fight. He rushed at Lusher and hit him on the shoulder.

"I shall take you into custody for being drunk and disorderly and assaulting me in the execution of my duty," said Lusher— and, as Caston replied, "It will take a better man than you," prepared to arrest him. Then someone struck Lusher from behind. He was pitched to the ground. John Caston stamped on his face and kicked him in the ribs. He drew his truncheon and struck Alfred on the arm. Roofe, who was standing behind, struck him across the shoulders with a whip-stalk, exclaiming "Don't use that damned thing!" Alfred came at him again, and whilst someone grabbed the constable from behind, wrested the truncheon from him whilst the crowd continually obstructed.

Someone took Alfred down Blyburgate towards the Black Boy, Lusher followed; another tussle ensued in which both fell, Alfred kicking and punching viciously. Lusher had almost succeeded in getting handcuffs on him, when John Caston again intervened, striking the constable on the face and kicking him on the knee.

At this point Charles Aldous came to Lusher's assistance, in spite of a threat from John— "If you touch me, I will poke you in the face." This threat, however, he did not carry out. And more help was at hand, for Inspector Lingley now arrived to assist Lusher and Aldous in arresting Alfred Caston. John was arrested soon afterwards.

When the case was heard at Beccles Police Court on May 21st, two witnesses testified for Roofe, and there being uncertainty about the identity of the man who struck Lusher with a whip, Roofe was acquitted. Alfred Caston— 28 days hard labour; John Caston 21 ditto.

On several other occasions in the course of the year the police had difficulty with obstreperous drunks. Local evidence was not wanting to support the claims of the Temperance Movement whose first Beccles Branch was formed in 1840 and had 220 members by 1845. In the 1890's the Band of Hope and the Church of England Temperance Society were both active; and they were joined in 1896 by the British Women's Temperance Association, at whose first annual general meeting in 1897 in the Primitive Methodist schoolroom an "American Tea Party" was held. Each member brought at least one shilling and told the meeting how the money had been obtained— begged, earned or saved. One member, instead of putting her washing out, did a little at home; the money thus saved, she spent in buying flour and meal, made bread, sold it to her friends and thus saved 8s 6d. Another dressed dolls and made babies' boots; she presented 5s. A young member bought bloaters and herrings and sold them to her friends; by this means, and raising a plant, she gave 2s. Another young member received by post 6d. from a gentleman she had induced to sign the pledge: she added 6d. as a thankoffering that she was still keeping the pledge herself. Others denied themselves chocolate, made dresses and bonnets, gathered flowers and sold them for buttonholes. One member told how she had been given money to buy stout, but had signed the pledge and saved the cash. There were lists of useful little kindnesses done for which pennies had been received. By the various means £3.1.0 was raised— part to be sent to the central B.W.T.A. fund and part to the Homes for Inebriate Women. The branch had begun the previous year with 12 members; now there were 100.

This was one of many Temperance efforts in the town throughout the year. Another, on Easter Monday, was an entertainment in the Town Hall which included a drama entitled "A Drunken Frolic" — "which met with general applause for the plainness of its temperance teaching."

An anecdote of the Jubilee year— of doubtful authenticity— was of a proposal made at a parish meeting that the permanent local memorial should be a brewery where the proposer and his friends should be able to enjoy free beer whenever they felt inclined. This inspired some light verse:

"How best can we exalt, you think,
These sixty years of glorious drink?...
For sixty years, be not befooled,
The Queen has reigned, but drink has ruled."

These lines might have brought a wry smile from a Beccles policeman.

13. MUSICAL CONVIVIALITY

WHAT SARTORIAL PREPARATIONS there must have been for the Fancy Dress Ball in February! Over a hundred ladies and gentlemen attended and the costumes, viewed from the gallery, "made one of the prettiest sights ever seen in the Town Hall". Mr Brundell as a masher, Mrs B. as a Chrysanthemum; the Messrs Algar as Buffalo Bill and Prince Charming, Miss Algar as a Poppy; Charles I and a Scotch lass, Lord Nelson and a milkmaid, a Russian Prince and a fairy godmother, a nigger and a Dutch peasant, a soldier bold, a Union Jack— these were some of the ingenious designs. Dancing continued until 4 a.m.

But music was the great source of entertainment. They were enthusiastic music-makers. "Entertainment" and "music" were almost synonymous. Here was one of two fields outside the home— "good works" was the other— in which women's talents were almost as much in demand as men's.

At the New Year's entertainment for the N.C.Os of the Volunteers, a "conversazione" was arranged instead of the usual monthly "smoker", so that ladies could be present and could contribute to the programme of vocal and instrumental music, interspersed with recitations, followed by dancing to a string band. The party ended at 1 a.m. Next week the Conservatives held a smoking concert (ladies in the gallery only) principally to hear a speech by the local M.P., H.S.Foster; songs and selections from Delf's band enlivened the evening. Indeed there was hardly a week, even in summer, without some musical entertainment, or some occasion with music, as on the following week, when the employees of the Great Eastern Railway held their annual dinner at the Falcon. Speeches and songs at the piano alternated. January closed with an evening of music by the choir of the Primitive Methodist Chapel and a concert in the

Town Hall with Edwyn Wolseley accompanied by Madam Anna Lang, "the celebrated Swedish violinist", a Musical Farce and Tableaux Vivants.

Beccles Orchestral Society, founded in 1895, held its first Concert of 1897 in February, with the assistance of five professionals— two singers and three instrumentalists. The orchestra consisted of four 1st and four 2nd violins, viola, three 'cellos, double bass, flute, oboe, two clarionets, cornet, euphonium, piano and harmonium. The music included pieces by Schumann, Haydn, Beethoven, Sullivan, German and Mendelssohn. The other principal event of February was a visit of "Madam Marie Levante's orchestra of Ladies and Concert Party", who gave performances on four successive evenings (a different programme for each)— admission 6d, 1s and 2s. The Town Hall was packed for the last performance, on Sunday evening.

Events in March included a Benefit Concert for Thomas Cocks, late Sergeant-Major of the Artillery Volunteers, who had been ill for three years. Proceeds £7.5.0.

The "Pleasant Sunday Afternoon Society", managed by members of the Congregational Church, but not exclusively denominational, was perhaps the most flourishing organisation in the town. It had 295 members (an increase of 24 on 1896) and sometimes had attendances of 350 at its meetings, where the entertainment included talks and recitations, but was predominantly musical, with male and female soloists. The Society had its own special excursion to London in August. At the A.G.M. in October, a speaker remarked: "When we look at society today, and think of the cleavage between workmen and employers, the selfishness, the monopolising spirit now so prevalent, there is great need for intelligent sympathy and earnest endeavour in order to bring in the reign of righteousness, justice and brotherly love. We hear of men proposing various remedies for the evils of the day, but there will never be a valid reason for the passing away of the Church or of such institutions as the P.S.A. There is no hope for the world in the transference of the resources of life from one class to another; the real need is the change in men's hearts." The tenor of this speech was quite different from most public speeches in Jubilee year. A collection was made at the end of the meeting for the Helping Hand for members in need.

Beccles Choral Society gave two concerts during the year. Mr Warder Harvey, Parish Organist, conducted. There were seven ladies in the orchestra of twenty-one. The Town Hall was full for the second concert when Haydn's "Creation" was performed with a chorus of eighty.

The enthusiasm for music was well exemplified at the Sale of Work in July at the Rectory Garden, in aid of the Church Missionary Society; for besides the usual things— the stalls of plain and fancy work, woollens, dolls, ices, sweets (the usual ladies of the parish presiding)— there was a long programme of music in the afternoon and selections by the Artillery Band in the evening.

Nor were public Dinners— those lengthy functions so popular with the Victorians— complete without songs. At the Dinner to the retiring Mayor, the greatest occasion of the civic year and the longest, the speeches (remarkable, even at a gathering such as this, for mutual congratulations and general back-slappings) were punctuated by songs— eleven of them, including such popular favourites as "The Village Blacksmith", "The Soldiers of the Queen", "The Gallants of England", "They all love Jack", "Sweethearts and Wives", "God Bless Victoria".

Lighter occasions, too, provided a happy excuse for a bit of a singsong, as when the members of the Corporation, and some others handy with a gun, met for the annual Rook Shooting (on the

Common). The rooks proving strong on the wing, the bag no more than some half score brace of birds, and dusk coming on, the party adjourned to an out-house on the plantation where the health of the Mayor was suitably pledged; and a few songs further enlivened the evening.

Music was cultivated in the schools. Two of the Girls' private schools arranged concerts in the Town Hall at the end of the Christmas term. The Waveney House concert, (in aid of the Hospital Fund) presenting a "School Jubilee Frolic", attracted an audience of 250. F.C.Oakley* recalled the informal musical evenings of the Glee Club at the Fauconberge School, and especially the jolly event at the end of the Summer term, when it was customary to sing a "horkey":

"We hev ploughed
We hev sown
We hev repp
We hev mown
We hev gott
In ther corn
Now we croy
HORKEY!"

"This triumphal finale would always find the head-master weak with laughter, and mopping his face with an outsize handkerchief."

Exuberant singing, however, did not always meet with universal approval:

AN ABOMINABLE NUISANCE

Sir,

Will you kindly allow me a small space in your valuable paper to express my grievance? The Old Market is made a concert-room three or four times a week, and especially every Saturday night—or rather Sunday morning—about twelve or half-past,

* *East Anglian Magazine* (August 1951)

by a crew of noisy fellows who seem to find amusement in disturbing respectable people by singing all the songs imaginable and mostly they are accompanied in their singing by a concertina. This is very annoying to hard-working people who expect to get a little rest after a hard week's work. Cannot our worthy officers of the law put a stop to this nuisance of singing, not to mention the coarse oaths and jests we get thrown in for nothing? Hoping you will oblige,

I remain, yours etc.
ONE OF THE ANNOYED

Juvenile carol-singers, too, were "not always acceptable to the parties serenaded, if one may judge from opening doors and flying figures".

Then there was Charlie Sheppard, tramp— one of those involved in the burglary at the jeweller's shop— who lodged at the Queen's Head and made a penny or two by singing and playing his tin whistle in the pubs.

Another popular musician was simple Charlie Took, who had served in the army abroad and had suffered from sunstroke. He could play a fiddle. On market days he would dress up— on his head a billycock hat decorated with ribbons and his trousers adorned with coloured ribboned garters— and, standing at some prominent place in the town, he would play from memory his repertoire of folk songs and dances. After the markets had closed, Charlie would "do" the public houses, a willing recipient of many free drinks from the appreciative audiences.

Thus there was music in abundance to suit all tastes, though support for the most ambitious musical enterprise of the year was disappointingly meagre. This was a series of lectures in the Town Hall by Arthur Hughes (son of the author of *Tom Brown's Schooldays*) on the music of Wagner. The parish organist and his wife, and Miss Boyce, daughter of the Headmaster of the Leman School, assisted at the piano; and Mr E.A.Abbott, who had recently settled in the town as a music teacher, played the violin. But Wagner was too strong or too strange musical meat for the townspeople.

And though music, in general, flourished, the drama did not. The theatre had been popular from the mid-eighteenth century until the 1840s, when the remarkable Fisher family closed its theatres in East Anglian towns. The Fishers had provided dramatic fare of high quality; no season was complete without at least one Shakespearean play. There was no Shakespeare in the 1890s.

Humour of the Year

TOO PERSONAL: *"How do you like your new governess, Dolly?" "Awfully much, papa. I love her. She's the nicest I ever had. Don't you love her, papa?"*

JEALOUSY: *Miss Charming: "Yes, I've had many a man kneel at my feet." Miss Envi: "I should stick to one chiropodist if I were you, dear!"*

CURIOUSLY ENOUGH *it is the loafers who do not care to work for their bread.*

A SON OF THE SOIL: *Tourist: "What is the soil like about here, my man?" Intelligent native: "Well, zur, when it rains that dew be very dirty!"*

A CORRECTION: *He: "I suppose you find a great many dull people here?" She: "On the contrary, it is always the dull people who find me."*

14. GOOD WORKS ABOUNDING

THERE DIED IN February a well-known local character, Billy Beane, the chimney-sweep, "the most repulsive creature I have ever seen. He hardly seemed human; more like half-man, half-monkey... his face was distinguishable from the rest of his person only by the whites of his eyes, as he flashed furtive glances from side to side." For long he was held up to children, though he was really of harmless disposition, as a kind of terror; and he had often been before the magistrates for drunkenness. He carried a bag of soot to show his calling, and into this he immediately deposited any food given to him. For years he had subsisted on charity.

An inquest was held in August on Charlotte Frankland, aged 87, widow of William Frankland, harness-maker. She lived by herself in a cottage in the Queen's Head Yard, off Newgate Street. Charles Brady, a labourer, of Newgate Street, said he looked after the deceased, without payment, and used sometimes to take his victuals and eat at hers, as she did not like to be alone. She could not get her meals for herself, so he used to get the things out for her. On Monday 2nd he went to her house. Though it was a hot day, she complained of the cold, so he lit a fire and got her some brandy. She felt a little better. He left her half an hour later. Soon afterwards a little girl came to tell him Mrs Frankland was unwell. It appeared she had fallen from her chair. He went for Mrs Copeman, who helped him to get the old lady to bed. Mrs Copeman stayed with her day and night until she died. The Coroner commented upon the great kindness Brady and the neighbours had shown; and the Jury, returning a verdict of "Accidental Death", concurred.

A third example of neighbourly charity was recorded in this brief notice: "THANKS. Widow

Hembling desires to return her heartfelt thanks to all who so generously assisted her last week by subscribing for a brief for obtaining a mangle to enable her to get a living."

Small acts of kindness and charity should have a place in local history, representing, as they truly do, the heart of social life, though largely unrecorded and scattered. There was, however, a focus of charitable effort in Beccles: the Hospital. Established by local subscription in 1874, it was a source of great pride. This letter shows how readily its welfare was connected with other things:

ELOCUTION CLASS— A SUGGESTION

Sir,

Permit me, through the medium of your esteemed paper, to suggest the formation of an advanced elocution class for ladies and gentlemen during the coming winter months. The services of some good professor— preferably one who understands a little of the technique of stage-craft— ought to be secured, and I feel pretty certain the scheme would turn out a success. At the close of the season a theatrical performance might be given in aid of the local hospital..."

Gifts to the Hospital were made every week, some in cash, more in kind, and this year included:

Five guineas from the Mayoress.
Ten pounds— proceeds of an entertainment.
Five pounds from Mrs Day.
Books, magazines, pictures, stereoscope and slides.
Butter, eggs, fruit, vegetables, flowers, plants.
Pheasants, partridges, ducks.
Flannel jackets, old linen, medicine bottles.
A self-propelled chair (proceeds of a concert).
A pair of crutches.
Church and Chapel collections.

Harvest Service collections from twenty villages.
Sweets, crackers, iced cakes, tea and pastries at Christmas

Besides these gifts, there were small collections from the Bakers, Bricklayers, Builders, Coach-builders, Gasfitters, Harness-makers, Police and eight other similar groups; School Collections; Boxes at the principal inns and the Coffee Rooms; Village Collections and Village Scholars collections; and the proceeds of two Promenade Concerts. In the list of donors and in the organisation of voluntary efforts for the Hospital, women were prominent.

Another charity which attracted wide support was the Soup Kitchen, to which over 200 people subscribed. It had been established in 1871 by the then Mayor, Joseph Mayhew. That it was still much needed in 1897 indicates the continuance of much winter distress.

Several schools helped in charitable work. The younger pupils of Bayfield High School held a small Sale of Work for the Hospital; the Beccles College Band played at the entertainment in the Town Hall on behalf of Dr Barnardo's Homes; the Fauconberge School held a concert, and in addition gave £13 for the maintenance of a child, for the Waifs and Strays Society.

In *A Record of the Crowfoots of Beccles*, H.W. Crowfoot comments thus upon E.B.Crowfoot (whose untimely death is referred to in "A Loss to the Town") and his sisters:

> I cannot think of him and his generation without recording how completely they spent their lives in serving their fellow men. They lived in the days before the Welfare State, and much of the work they did for nothing is now done by highly trained and well-paid officials. In common with many ladies of leisure of the Victorian era, my aunts spent themselves in good works. They each

> had a district where they visited all and sundry. Auntie Mary's district was known to us as "The Back Street". Its more respectable name was Newgate. We irreverently said it was so called because that was where some of its less respectable inhabitants were sent. Our aunts' lives centred in the church. They seldom missed the week-day services and took an active part in the Sunday School, as did my father, who even on his busiest days found time to teach a class of boys.

A more detailed account of "Aunt Mary" follows:

> I can see her now as we bade her goodnight, standing with some new book in one hand and her bedroom candlestick in the other, reading, reading far into the night, oblivious of time, until I suppose the candle warned her that bed-time had come. Works of a philosophical nature and serious Reviews, such as the Hibbert Journal, were of special interest to her, though often as much for the opposition aroused in her mind as for the new currents of thought they set in motion.

H.W.Crowfoot then quotes from a friend who wrote of Mary Crowfoot:

> I remember how, when her activities were at their height, including as they did deep reading, Sunday School and district work, Bible Class, Boys' Club, wood-carving and fret-work, a sewing class for girls held at 7 a.m. on Saturday morning, the working for and holding an annual sale of work for the Delhi Zanana Mission, gardening and the care of a large house, she would yet find time to devote to us, as children, when we came to stay in Beccles, and delight us with her energy, her earnestness, her reading.

The names of Mary Crowfoot and her sister, and

other members of the family were to be found on all subscription lists for local causes. Thus on the Beccles National School list for 1897 we find:

Crowfoot Miss E.	1. 0. 0
Crowfoot Miss M.	1. 0. 0
Crowfoot Mrs J.R.	5. 0. 0
Crowfoot Messrs	5. 0. 0

And the sisters contributed £2.10.0 each to the fund for the Jubilee Nurses' Home.

Humour of the Year

JACK: *"Mother, where do flies come from?" Mother: "God makes them, Jackie dear." Jack (after a long pause): "What a fiddling job it must be!"*

AUNTIE: *"Is that the Miss Steel who's going to be married, Elsie?" Elsie: "Yes, Auntie. But she must have needed a deal of persuading, because I heard the clergyman on Sunday say it was the third time he'd asked her."*

THE SUNDAY GAME: *Fond Mother: "O Peter, Peter, I thought I told you not to play with your soldiers on Sunday!" Peter: "But I call them the Salvation Army on Sunday."*

EEFIE: *(after witnessing her first christening) "Mummie, do they water them to make them grow?"*

15. ROUGH SURGERY FOR THE RURAL POOR

WHEN AUGUSTUS JESSOPP asserted that "The East Anglian is, of all the inhabitants of these islands, most wanting in natural courtesy, in delicacy of feeling, or in anything remotely resembling romantic sentiment", he provoked much indignation. But he supported his claim with some amusing illustrations, like this anecdote of a wheelwright and his apprentice. Whilst using both hands on a job, the lad had some nails ready in his mouth and inadvertently swallowed one. He thought he should tell his master, and did so. "That's all right, boy" the wheelwright replied, "there's plenty more nails in the box." Sometimes, however, indifference or callousness by those in authority did not pass without public protest.

When village gossip is prompted by indignation, strange stories will be put about. Sometimes they may be substantially true. The treatment of old William Gray of Geldeston was a case in point.

There was a large attendance of Guardians of the Loddon and Clavering Union at Heckingham Workhouse on October 18th, when, after routine business, an enquiry into the case was opened. Gray had been suffering from a diseased leg and was receiving medical relief from the Guardians. He had been attended by Dr Helsham, of Beccles, one of the Board's officers.

Mr Mower, Guardian for Geldeston, spoke first, alleging there was a grave scandal in the parish and neighbourbood about the way Dr Helsham had performed the operation on Gray's leg. In severing the bone of the leg, he had used a rusty and worn-out saw— "In my opinion," Mower declared, "it was not fit to saw wood with." Nor had the doctor bothered to consult the patient or his wife about performing the operation.

At this point, Gray's wife and a Mrs Baker, who was attending Gray during his illness, were called into the Board Room to give evidence.

Mrs Gray said the operation was performed on her husband on Saturday, September 11th. Both she and her daughter had to complain of the way it was done. The saw Dr Helsham used was old and rusty, and it was picked up on the heath in the village where it had been thrown away as useless. The doctor never asked her consent nor her husband's and she had had no idea he intended to remove the foot. He did not see the limb again for nearly a fortnight. A portion of the diseased bone was now protruding from the flesh, which would probably necessitate a second operation.

In reply to a question, Mrs Gray said Dr Helsham had usually been kind to her husband. She had no other cause for complaint.

Mrs Baker was called next. She stated that she had been present at the operation and held the patient's leg while it was done. (The saw was now produced, and handed round the room for the Guardians' inspection). Dr Helsham cut away the fleshy portions of the leg with a razor which she found for him in the house. No chloroform was administered. When the doctor asked her if she could find a saw, he said, "Any old thing will do. I only want it for a minute. Put some grease on it." Except for scissors, he had no instruments with him. She thought the "jar" from the saw must have caused Gray considerable pain, as he shrieked loudly several times. The foot was mortified and had been in that condition for some time. After the operation, Dr Helsham threw the foot into the hearth, and she subsequently took it into the churchyard and buried it. Before the doctor left he put some ointment on the leg and gave her instuctions as to doing it up. He did not see the limb again for a fortnight.

Dr Helsham was now called in. The statements made by witnesses were read to him and he admitted them to be mainly correct. He said the case was one of gangrene of the leg and described in detail the progress of the disease. He had had only five cases in his experience. They had to be dealt with cautiously as the wounds were highly infectious. An operation was impossible until the disease had reached a certain point. On Friday, September 10th, he went to see Gray, thinking it was time something more should be done to the leg, and made an appointment to call the next day. He did so, but had no surgical instruments with him, except a pocket case, as he expected to do no more than remove some dead skin or flesh and dress the leg again. He removed as much of the putrid flesh as he could with a razor which was in the house. Then, to his astonishment, he found that the bone was affected and that the foot would have to be amputated at once. He chose the oldest saw that could be found in order that it might be at once destroyed; the matter adhering to it from the leg would be highly infectious. With regard to his not telling Gray or his wife of his intention, he said this was not customary in all cases. Mrs Gray suffered from a weak heart, and it might have upset her. In reply to the Chairman, Dr Helsham said he saw no reason why the saw should not have been used for that purpose, though he admitted it was not a surgical instrument. (Laughter).

This concluded the evidence. Dr Helsham withdrew and the Board discussed the case. Several members spoke in favour of the doctor and a resolution was proposed and seconded: "That the Board, having heard the statements of both parties, do not consider it necessary to move a vote of censure on Dr Helsham."

The resolution by no means satisfied many members. "A lengthy and somewhat heated discussion took place"— the local newspaper's discretion in giving no details is a loss to the local historian. An amendment was eventaully moved by a Dissenting minister: "That this Board, having heard the statements of both parties, do not consider it necessary to formally censure Dr Helsham, but, at the same time, the Board regrets that he went to the patient's house knowing some serious operation would in all probability be necessary and neglected to take his proper instruments with him." The voting was: Amendment 24, Resolution 5.

The parties were called in and informed of the decision by the Chairman. Dr Helsham immediately tendered his resignation. He refused to attend Gray again during the remaining term of his office but promised to assist, if required, in the choice of a successor.

Second thoughts, however, prevailed. The Board met again on November 1st, when a letter from the doctor was read, requesting to be allowed to withdraw his resignation, which he had tendered assuming the Board wished it and not fully understanding the wording of the amended resolution of October 18th. The Board assented unanimously to the withdrawal of the resignation.

Humour of the Year

A PERFECT TREASURE: *Mistress: "Now, you must always sweep well behind the doors, Mary." Mary: "Yes'm, trust me for that; it's the only way we can get the dust out of sight."*

REASONABLE: *"Bridget, there's a serviette missing!" "Yes, mum. I've taken it to boil the pudding in." "Boil the pudding in!" "Well, mum, it was only the dirty one."*

16. THE LOCAL ELECTION: A SEQUEL

ON NOVEMBER 1st a local election was due. The four retiring members of the Council all offered themselves for re-election; and the question was: would the voting reflect the apparently widespread annoyance felt at the selection in January of Councillor Woodroffe's son as Town Surveyor, or would the lapse of nearly ten months and the popularity of the young man as captain of the highly sucessful Beccles Caxton XI lead to different feelings?

The retiring members were: N.W.Pells (the Mayor), C.P.Poll, H.Woolner and— T.A.Woodroffe!

The week before the election, three letters in the *East Suffolk Gazette* reminded the burgesses of January's events. The first letter referred to remarks made by Councillor Poll when the Council considered, and rejected, the memorial requesting the rescinding of young Woodroffe's appointment. At the same meeting, Councillor Woolner also had spoken emphatically against the memorial.

Dear Sir,

In view of the approaching contest at Beccles, it is only right, I think, that the insulting words used by one of the retiring members at the Council meeting of February 22nd last, when a certain question was being discussed, should be brought to the notice of the electors, especially as that member is now seeking to know "them" without their going to his "shop". The member is reported to have said "The memorial is signed by less than 200 persons. Who are they? If they came into my shop tomorrow, I should not know them. What have they at stake?"

In reply, a Councillor reminded him that "They all had votes." These votes Mr Poll would now like to secure; but, in face of the insult to them, it is now the electors' turn to say "We do not know him", and give their votes to other candidates.

Yours etc.
AN ELECTOR

Dear Mr Editor,

I trust you won't forget to remind your readers of the 'affair of the Surveyor', in connection with the coming election. It would be a good time for them to show by their votes what they thought of that piece of jobbery.

I am, dear sir, Yours respectfully
A FOND BUT THICK-SKINNED PARENT

And a third letter on the same theme was signed "NEMESIS".

An unprecedented number of ten candidates came forward, showing the unusual interest in the contest, though somewhat confusing to the voters.

Various conveyances were used to take voters to the Town Hall. Mr McQueen, councillor and prominent draper, sent out his pony and cart to pick up for the retiring councillors, and two of the new contenders had similar support.

Up to 12 o'clock only about 200 voters had been registered, but the dinner hour brought in another 150; and in the evening activity became so much brisker that during the last half-hour the arrangements proved entirely inadequate. A few people, unable to get into the station before 8 p.m., could not record their votes. During this excitement, there took place an incident described by the paper as "disgusting". Mr E.Cracknell, licensee of the Angel, had driven up a voter, and his horse and cart were standing opposite the Town Hall when another conveyance came up, whose horse's collar became entangled with Cracknell's cart. Some spectators pulled back the horse, but the irritated publican "spoke out" (his words were not printed, and may have been unprintable). A man named Howell then taunted Cracknell, who jeeringly enquired, "If I put my nose into your mouth, will you bite it?" Howell said he would, Cracknell pushed his head forward, Howell snapped at his nose and bit a piece off. This incident "roused a laugh from the crowd." The injured man betook himself to the police station.

Soon after this, polling ended. A crowd assembled between nine and ten for the declaration, which was as follows:

Elected: Pells 459; Woodroffe 358; Copeman 282;
Revell 276.

Not elected: Mickleburgh 252; Jolly 141;
Spaull 141; Block 114; Poll 77;
Woolner 32.

The re-election of the Mayor had been a foregone conclusion. He had fulfilled the duties of his office, in an unusually arduous and difficult year, to the general satisfaction. The re-election of Woodroffe, well ahead of all the others, was more surprising. But the abysmal showing of Poll and Woolner was an obvious sequel to January's events. Hell knows no fury like local electors insulted.

Yet only 830 burgesses had voted, though the number on the roll was 1350. After all the fuss, the customary apathy had not been dispelled.

Small Advertisements: Christmas

DURRANT'S AUCTION MART, BECCLES. *The next Sale will be on Friday, December 17th and will be the* ANNUAL SALE OF CHRISTMAS MEAT.

ENGLISH HOTHOUSE *and other Grapes, Pines, Oranges, Nuts of all kinds. Figs, Muscatels, and other Christmas Fruit.* LARGE STOCK OF MISTLETOE. *T.J.Self, New Market Place, Beccles.*

MONEY EASILY MADE. *All Shopkeepers and others can make large profits by sending for our Grand-Value Parcels of* CHRISTMAS CARDS. *Our Selections at 1/6, 2/9, and 5/6 carriage paid, contain only cards which sell readily at from 2d to 6d each...*